FRANK DWIGHT BALDWIN, M. H.,
Major General U. S. Army.

MICHIGAN MILITARY RECORDS

THE D. A. R. OF MICHIGAN HISTORICAL COLLECTIONS:
RECORDS OF THE REVOLUTIONARY SOLDIERS BURIED
IN MICHIGAN; THE PENSIONERS OF TERRITORIAL
MICHIGAN; AND THE SOLDIERS OF MICHIGAN
AWARDED THE "MEDAL OF HONOR"

By SUE IMOGENE SILLIMAN,
State Historian, D. A. R. of Michigan.

WITH AN ADDED FOREWORD

by the

MICHIGAN HISTORICAL COMMISSION

CLEARFIELD

Originally Published As
Michigan Historical Commission
Bulletin No. 12
Lansing, 1920

Reprinted with a Foreword by the
Michigan Historical Commission
Genealogical Publishing Company
Baltimore, 1969

Reprinted for
Clearfield Company, Inc., by
Genealogical Publishing Co., Inc.
Baltimore, Maryland
1996

International Standard Book Number 0-8063-0312-3
Library of Congress Catalogue Card Number 79-80642

Reprinted with Permission

Foreword

Since the publication of *Michigan Military Records* in 1920, many pertinent military books have been published, and valuable manuscripts and official records have been located. Yet, Sue Imogene Silliman's book remains a necessary tool to serious historical and genealogical research.

In 1929 Volume XL of the *Michigan Pioneer Collections* was published, containing many documents of the War of 1812. Alec Gilpin's *War of 1812 in the Old Northwest* (Ann Arbor: University of Michigan Press, 1958) is useful and contains an extensive bibliography. Hundreds of territorial documents were printed in James E. Carter (ed.), *Territorial Papers of the United States: Michigan*, Volumes X, XI, XII (Washington: Government Printing Office, 1942, 1943, 1945). A quarterly that contains much genealogical material to fit in with Silliman's book is *Michigan Heritage*, published in Kalamazoo.

The best manuscript military records are in the National Archives, Washington, D. C.; completed Form 288 enables the National Archives to trace many Revolutionary and War of 1812 veterans. These records often contain information about length of service, pension applications, and residence after leaving the service.

In Michigan the most useful manuscript depository is the Michigan Historical Commission Archives, Lansing. This institution has some Black Hawk War and Patriot War records and extensive records of Civil War regiments. The Civil War records contain such details as physical descriptions of veterans, length and places of service, and mustering out information.

When used with the printed and manuscript records, Silliman's *Michigan Military Records* can be a valuable research aid.

MICHIGAN HISTORICAL COMMISSION
February, 1969

PREFACE

TO collect scattered data of events long passed, and to compile them into form so that they can be of service to the present and future generations is to add to the sum of human knowledge, and to make a distinct contribution to the study of history.

Such a task requiring talent, patience, and perseverance has been undertaken by Miss Sue I. Silliman, State Historian, of the Daughters of the American Revolution of Michigan, in becoming Editor of this volume,—*Michigan Military Records compiled by the Daughters of the American Revolution of Michigan.*

The compilation of names and data of "Revolutionary Soldiers Buried in Michigan" was commenced by another talented Daughter of Michigan and a former State Historian of the Daughters of the American Revolution of Michigan, Mrs. Lillian Drake Avery. The Chapters of the Daughters of the American Revolution of Michigan which have located and marked many of these graves in Michigan have co-operated with Mrs. Avery and Miss Silliman in furnishing data regarding these men of the American Revolution who immigrated as pioneers to Michigan.

For the Chapters on "Territorial Pensioners" and "Congressional Medal of Honor Men of Michigan" we are wholly indebted to Miss Silliman. Until she gave herself so wholeheartedly to this task, there were no such lists within the borders of our State. With the list of "Territorial Pensioners" is a brief digest of the Pension Laws prior to 1836.

The names of all Medal of Honor Men have been published by the United States Government, but not by States, so the work of compiling the names, and data of the "Medal of Honor Men" of Michigan necessitated examining not only a list of names of more than three thousand men, who have received this decoration, but also the names of their battalions in order to learn from the battalion names what "Medal of Honor Men" belonged to Michigan.

Beginning with General Alexander Macomb, Michigan's first Medal of Honor man, more than sixty Michigan soldiers have been decorated with this medal which is awarded, by the Congress of the United States, for valor and heroism in action. It is treasured by holders more than all other possessions because it is the highest decoration awarded by the United States Government.

Of the hundreds of men who have been thus decorated, only four soldiers have had this much coveted medal bestowed upon them twice. Of these four men, two were Michigan men, Lt. Thomas W. Custer; and Major General Frank Dwight Baldwin, now Adjutant General of Colorado.

Miss Silliman's investigation includes biographical data, the ground of award, and military record. It shows for Michigan a fine heritage of patriotism and bravery and is particularly valuable coming at the present-day history-in-the-making.

The Daughters of the American Revolution of Michigan gratefully acknowledge their indebtedness to Miss Silliman for the honor she has bestowed upon them, by doing this work as their State Historian; and they wish also to convey to the Michigan Historical

Commission their pleasure that the book is published
under the auspices of the Commission.

Mrs. WILLIAM HENRY WAIT,
State Regent, Daughters of
the American Revolution of
Michigan.

Ann Arbor, Michigan.
December 18, 1918.

INTRODUCTION

THE D. A. R. of Michigan Historical Records are being compiled as a patriotic duty to the State whose sons and daughters glory in her history. The Daughters of the American Revolution, proud of the military records of the stalwart sons of the State, desire to supply authentic data, easily accessible, to those who may not know Michigan's rich heritage of valor.

Though the records are incomplete, their publication became necessary that those doing historical research for data concerning the Revolutionary war need not duplicate the records which have been filed.

Chapter one is a compilation of biographical and genealogical data, from memoranda filed with the State historian, by the chapters of the State, concerning the Revolutionary soldiers buried in Michigan—whose graves have been officially located, or marked by the D. A. R. This work was begun under the direction of Mrs. Lillian Drake Avery, past State Historian, D. A. R. The material furnished by the chapters to the present historian has been compiled and annotated, —the annotations are based on the *Michigan Historical Collections*, and the muster rolls of New York, New Jersey, Pennsylvania and Vermont.

Chapter two contains the names and pension records of soldiers who were residents of Michigan Territory; and is compiled from the "Pension Establishment" records of 1836—a work recommended by G. M. Saltzgabt, U. S. Commissioner of Pensions, Washington, and secured through the courtesy of Mr. W. W. Bishop, Librarian of the University of Michigan.

Chapter three, Michigan "Medal of Honor" Men, is based on the Government publications of 1904 and 1910; Report of Board of Officers on Medal of Honor Recommendations; and, Medals of Honor issued by the War Department; the circular by the Judge-Advocate-General; and records copied from the Adjutant-General's office, by Mr. M. H. Bumphrey, of Washington, D. C., to whom the D. A. R. of Michigan are indebted for many other valuable records.

The Compiler is also greatly indebted to the State Historical Commission; Mr. W. H. Shumaker and Claude H. Phelps, Three Rivers; Mrs. Mary C. Spencer, State Librarian; Mrs. Lillian D. Avery; the State Board and Chapters of the D. A. R. of Michigan for their kindly co-operation.

SUE I. SILLIMAN,

State Historian, D. A. R. of Michigan, 1917–1920.

February 1, 1920,
Three Rivers, Michigan.

CONTENTS

ILLUSTRATIONS

———

REVOLUTIONARY SOLDIERS BURIED IN MICHIGAN, Whose Graves Have Been Officially Reported, Located, Or Marked By The Daughters Of The American Revolution Of Michigan.

CHAPTER I

REVOLUTIONARY SOLDIERS BURIED IN MICHIGAN

EBENEZER ANNABIL

ANNABIL (also Annabell), Ebenezer. Born 1756. Died Sept. 23, 1842; buried at Bridgewater Center, Mich.; grave marked May, 1908, by Sarah Caswell Angell chapter, Ann Arbor.

Names of descendants:—Grandsons, Delos Mills and Hiram Mills of Bridgewater, Mich.; great-granddaughter, Mrs. Ira Van Geirson.

Revolutionary service:—A sergeant, served through the Revolution.

Data furnished by Sarah Caswell Angell chapter, Ann Arbor.

Ed. note:—Ebenezer Anna*ble* was a pensioner; see also Pensioners of Territorial Michigan.

ARCHIBALD ARMSTRONG

ARMSTRONG, Archibald. Born 1749.

Buried in Oakwood cemetery, Saline, Mich.; grave located by Ypsilanti chapter, Ypsilanti, Mich.

Revolutionary service:—A drummer boy in battles of Monmouth, N. J., June 28, 1778; Germantown, Pa., Oct. 4, 1777; Cowpens, S. C., Jan. 17, 1781; drummed the death march of Major André and aided in the final salute to victory at the surrender of Cornwallis.

Data recorded by Mrs. Georgiania Webb Owen, Ypsilanti.

Ed. note:—See also Pensioners of Territorial Michigan.

NATHANIEL BALDWIN

BALDWIN, Nathaniel. Born at Goshen, Conn., July 20, 1761.

Died Aug. 30, 1840; buried at Rochester, Mich.; grave marked, July 29, 1909, by General Richardson chapter, Pontiac.

Son of Nathaniel Baldwin.

Married Susanah Sherman, niece of Roger Sherman, a "Signer"; Mrs. Baldwin died June 2, 1839, aged 74.

Children:—John, Martha Minot, Nathaniel Augustus, Susanna Eliza, Walter, Sherman, Zimri. Living descendant recorded, 1912, Mrs. Milo Newberry, Oakland Co., Mich.

Place of residence before coming to Michigan, East Bloomfield, New York.

Revolutionary Service:—Enlisted in sixth regiment from Conn., under Col. Parsons "On duty July 17, 1775 at New London; discharged Dec. 10, 1775."

Came to Michigan, 1817; located two miles south of Rochester, Oakland Co., Mich.; entered land, 1819.

Authorities quoted:—*Mich. Hist. Colls.* III, 569; XXXIX, 437; *Baldwin Genealogy; Hist. of Oakland County,* I, ch. 6.

Ed. note:—See also Pensioners of Territorial Michigan.

ELI BALL

BALL, Eli. Born at Brookfield, Mass., Aug. 5, 1766.

Died Dec. 11, 1857; buried Whig Center cemetery, near Herricksville, Branch Co., Mich.; grave located, July 4, 1918, by Charity Cook chapter, Homer.

Children:—Elisha; Polly, married Simonds, second, Rogers; Anna, married Rev. Spear; Hannah, married Smith Jones.

Revolutionary Service:—"Military History of Eli Ball,
a soldier of the Revolutionary war:—Date of enlistment, June 8, 1782 to the fall of 1783; served continuously. Rank, private, under Capt. William
Mills, and Col. Brooks, 7th regiment of Mass. Date
of application for pension, May 6, 1839. Claim
allowed. Residence at date of application, Eckford,
Calhoun Co., Mich. Age at date of application, 72
yrs., 9 mo.; born Aug. 5, 1766, at Brookfield, Mass.
Pension record.

Residence:—"In 1840 Eli Ball lived at Clarendon, Calhoun Co., Mich.; in 1855 in Butler, Branch Co.,
Mich.

"The descriptive list of enlisted men in *Soldiers and
Sailors of Mass.*, dated Feb. 20, 1782, gives age,
seventeen; complexion, dark; hair dark; occupation farmer; enlistment three years."

Came to Michigan in the "thirties"; lived with his
children.

Authorities quoted:—Pension records; G. M. Saltz-
gabt, U. S. Comm. of Pensions; *Mass. Soldiers and
Sailors*, I, 536; Mrs. Anna Moore, granddaughter and
Geo. McDonnald, Quincy, Mich.

Data recorded by Mrs. Wm. H. Cortright, Homer,
Mich.

JAMES BANCKER

BANCKER, James.

Buried in the Farmer's Creek cemetery, Lapeer; grave
marked by General Richardson chapter, Pontiac,
Oct. 28, 1907.

Authorities quoted:— *History of Oakland County*
(Mich.), I, ch. 6.

JOHN BARBER

BARBER, John.   Born in Massachusetts, Sept. 19, 1757.
Died at Adrian, Mich., June 24, 1840, buried at Oak-
  wood, Adrian; grave marked, May 25, 1911, by the
  Lucy Wolcott Barnum chapter, Adrian.
Children:—John, b. June 15, 1792, m. Laura; Nancy, b.
  June 3, 1803, m. 1st, Paul Park, 2nd, Abram Critten-
  den; Selina, b. Sept. 5, 1807, m. Wm. Davis Burnall.
Revolutionary Service:—Enlisted Aug. 9, 1779; served
  as private in Capt. Abner Hayard's company, 2nd
  reg., commanded by Col. John Baily; name on
  "Honor Roll", dated at West Point, July 22, 1780.
Came to Michigan about 1837; located at Adrian.
Data recorded by Mrs. Frank P. Dodge, Adrian, Mich.

JONATHAN BARRON

BARRON, Jonathan.   Born at Reading, Mass., June
  30, 1760.
Died Dec. 2, 1834; buried in Hillsdale cemetery, St.
  Clair, Mich.; grave marked, May 30, 1904, by the
  Ot-Si-Ke-Ta chapter, St. Clair.
Son of Capt. Timothy Barron.
Jonathan Barron married Thankful Minor.
Names recorded of descendants living in St. Clair
  (1915):—William, George, Liela.
Revolutionary Service:—Enlisted in service under his
  father, a captain of the New Hampshire militia;
  was present at the battle of Bennington, Vt., Aug.
  16, 1777.
Places of residence:—Bath, N. H.; St. Clair, Mich.
Came to Michigan, 1813.
Occupation:—Farmer.

Data filed by the Ot-Si-Ke-Ta chapter, St. Clair.
Ed. note:—See also Pensioners of Territorial Michigan.

CALEB BATES

BATES, Caleb. Born at Boston, Mass.
Died, 1845; buried Lakeview cemetery, Hillsdale, Mich.;
grave marked, May 30, 1912, by Ann Gridley chapter,
Hillsdale.
Son of Benjamin and Hulda (Cudworth) Bates.
Married Mary Wilbur, b. July 1, 1767; d. at Hillsdale,
1811.
Children:—Mary, b. 1787; Caleb, Jr., b. 1788; Rebecca,
b. Jan. 21, 1797; Charlotte, b. Jan. 21, 1797; Joshua,
b. June 15, 1795; Electa, b. Dec. 8, 1799; Relief;
Lydia; Edith.
Revolutionary Service:—Enlisted, July 9, 1780, as a
private in Col. Wm. Shepard's reg.; discharged Dec.
13, 1780.
"Took up land, 1834; located at Hillsdale, 1835."
Occupation:—Farmer.
Data recorded by Mrs. O. J. Cornell, 58 S. Manning St.,
Hillsdale.
Ed. note:—From the letter files of Mrs. Wm. H. Wait,
State Regent, it is found that Benjamin Bates was a
private in Capt. Benj. Bonny's company of Col.
Ezra May's regiment. (2)—Caleb Bates was acci-
dentally killed by one of the first trains passing
through Hillsdale. In a letter signed Elva H. Wil-
loughby, the death of Caleb B. is given as occurring
"in his seventy-ninth year."

JONATHAN BEACH

BEACH, Jonathan. (Deacon.) Born at Goshen, Conn., Oct. 2, 1761.
Died, "1850 at the advanced age of ninety"; buried at Mt. Morris cemetery, Genesee County.
Son of Deacon Edmund and Mary (Deming) Beach.
Married Lucy Baldwin, dau. of Samuel and Mercy (Stanley) Baldwin.
Children[1]:—Erastus, b. July 24, 1786; Wait; Lucy; Harlow; Asahel; Lumen; Elisha; Seth. *Mich. Hist. Colls.*, XXI, 382.
Places of residence:—Green Co., N. Y.; Mt. Morris, N. Y.; Genesee Co., Mich.
Revolutionary Service:—Aide to Gen. Washington. Served in Col. Sheldon's 6th brigade for the defense of sea coast and frontier, 1780; in 1781, under Capt. Mathew Smith in Gen. Waterbury's state brigade. Joined Washington at Phillipsburg.
Came to Michigan, Sept. 1835, with his son Wait; located on the "Todd" farm which was later surveyed and platted and is now the third ward of Flint. The farmhouse was a log tavern and stood on the site of the River House.
Occupation:—Blacksmith in early life, later a farmer.
Authorities quoted:—Geo. H. Hazelton's *Reminiscences; Mich. Hist. Colls.*, XXI, 382; Henry M. Curtis, "History of the Presbyterian Church of Flint", in *Mich. Hist. Colls.*, XIII, 410.
Data recorded by General Richardson chapter, Pontiac, Mich.

---

1. The names of the children as recorded by Mrs. Lillian D. Avery, are:—Erastus, Alvin, Lydia, Ebenezer, Elisha, Harlow, Seth, Luman, Wait, Asahel Hooker, Lucy,

HOOPER BISHOP

BISHOP, Hooper. Born March 22, 1762.
Died April 3, 1861; buried in Novi cemetery, Oakland
Co., Mich.; grave marked Oct. 3, 1914, by General
Richardson chapter of Pontiac.
Married Betsey ——— b. March 22, 1758; d. Jan. 1,
1825.
Children:—Prudence, b. Sept. 3, 1794; Sally, b. Feb.
26, 1797, d. Feb. 4, 1858; Levi, b. June 8, 1799, d.
Oct. 18, 1870 at Novi; William, b. Nov. 21, 1802.
Revolutionary Service:—A private in Capt. John Car-
penter's company enlisted June 25, 1779; discharged
Sept. 25, 1779; served three mo. with the guards at
Springfield. Enlisted Oct., 1779 in Capt. Caleb
Keep's company under Col. Israel Chapen; discharged Nov. 21, 1779; enlisted for three mo., served
one mo., 11 days. Hooper Bishop's name occurs on
the South Brimfield descriptive list of men raised to
reinforce the Continental army for the term of six
months. "18 yrs., stature 5 ft., 5 in.; complexion
dark; residence South Brimfield; arrived in Springfield, July 11, 1780, marched to camp, July 11, 1780,
under command of Capt. Geo. Webb". In a list of
men raised for six months service and returned by
Brig. Gen. Patterson as having passed muster. The
return dated Oct. 25, 1780, at Camp Toloway; on
the pay-roll for the men raised by town of South
Brimfield, for six months service during 1780.
"Marched July, 1780, discharged Dec., 1780" at
West Point. Hooper Bishop, private in Capt. Abel
Kind's company, Col. Sear's regiment; enlisted Aug.
20, 1781, discharged Nov. 26, 1781, service three
months at Saratoga.

Came to Michigan about 1840; lived with son Levi Bishop near Novi.

Authorities quoted:—*Mass. Soldiers and Sailors*, II, 78; *History of Oakland County*, I, 90; *Mich. Hist. Colls.*, XXXIX, 453.

Data recorded by Mrs. Lillian Drake Avery, Pontiac, Mich.

JOHN BLANCHARD

BLANCHARD, John.   Born 1763.

Children:—David; Sophia Laqui (or Lakey).

Places of residence:—Meredith, Delaware Co., N. Y.; White Lake, Mich.; and Farmington, Oakland Co., Mich.

Revolutionary Service:—The name of John Blanchard is given as a pensioner in 1840, aged 77.   Residence, White Lake.

Came to Oakland Co., before 1834.

Authorities quoted:—*History of Oakland County*, ch. 6, p. 93.

Data recorded by Mrs. Lillian D. Avery, Pontiac.

Ed. note:—See also Pensioners of Territorial Michigan.

HUGH BRADY

BRADY, Hugh, Major-General, U. S. A.   Born in [2]Huntington Co., Pa., July, 1768.

Died at Detroit, Apr. 15, 1851; buried at Elmwood, Detroit.

Son of Capt. John and Mary Brady.   Capt. John Brady was a noted Indian fighter and while serving in the 12th Pa., was killed by the Indians.

Married.

---

2.   Also given as Northumberland Co.

Children:—Sarah; Preston.

Places of residence:—Northumberland Co., Pa.; Hunt-
ington Co., Pa.; Cumberland Co., Pa.; Detroit,
Mich.

Revolutionary Service:—Served in the revolution,
doing a boy's heroic part. "Many a day I walked
beside my brother John while plowing, carrying my
rifle in one hand and a forked stick in the other."
—The one for the Indians or Tories, the other to
clean the plow. Hugh's brother, carrying provisions
to his father, Capt. John Brady, smuggled a musket
along and so his father found him attached to the
company during an encounter with the enemy. The
mother worked beside her boys in the fields, sharing
their watch and danger. Hugh entered service
March 7th, 1792 and served in the western expedition under Gen. Wayne after the defeat of Gen. St.
Clair; Sept. 4th, 1792, in the 4th sub legion; made
lieut., Feb., 1794; Jan. 8, 1799, captain of the 10th
inf.; resigned in 1800; reappointed in 1808 by Pres.
Jefferson; July 6, 1812, appointed colonel of the 22nd
infantry and displayed the greatest bravery in the
hard fought battle of Chippewa. Distinguished
himself for bravery at Lundy's Lane and Niagara;
was wounded in each engagement. In 1822 was
made brevet brigadier-general for faithfulness in
service. In 1835 he was placed in command of the
department with headquarters at Detroit and during
the Canadian troubles he greatly aided in the preservation of peace on the frontier. May 30, 1848,
received the brevet rank of major-general for long
and faithful service.

Authorities quoted:—Gen. Wayne's *Orderly Book; Red-
book of Michigan*, 1871; *Appleton's Cyclopedia of*

*Amer. Biog.; Historical Register and Dict. of U. S. A.,
Mich. Hist. Colls.*
Data compiled from the above authorities by Sue I.
Silliman, Three Rivers.

JOHN BRITTON

BRITTON, John. Born at Long Island, 1755.
Died June, 1846 "of old age"; buried in Horton ceme-
tery, Atlas Twp. two and one-half miles south of
Atlas, Genesee Co.; grave marked, Nov. 6, 1917,
by the Genesee chapter of Flint.
Married Isabel Rice of Dublin, Ireland, who died 1809;
2nd w. Lydia Pipps Harris.
Children: — Elizabeth; Rebecca and Mary, twins;
Daniel; William; John.
Places of residence:—Gettysburg, Adams Co., Pa.;
Cayuga Co., N. Y.
The only data recorded with State historian, D. A. R.
concerning parentage of John B., states that the
"father was born in England and the mother in
Wales."
Revolutionary Service:—Served in Canada 1775-6; in
battle of Germantown, Pa., Oct. 4, 1777. "A private
in Capt. Geo. Forepaugh's co., 5th battalion, Phila-
delphia militia; in the battle of Monmouth, N. J.,
June 28, 1778."
Came to Michigan in 1842; located in Atlas Twp.,
Genesee Co., Mich.
Occupation:—Farmer and ironer.
Authorities quoted:—*Pennsylvania Archives*, fifth series;
Oakland County Gazette.

Data recorded by Genesee chapter, D. A. R. of Flint in 1916, by Miss Anna Grow of Atlas; and in 1918 by Mrs. G. E. Pomeroy of Flint.

AHIRA BROOKS

BROOKS, Ahira. Born March 10, 1760. Died April 20, 1858; buried first in the "old" cemetery, later moved to the "Soldiers cemetery", Sturgis, Mich.; grave located by the Abiel Fellows chapter, D. A. R., Three Rivers, Mich. Married Sarah ————, b. 1771; d. Aug. 26, 1848. Revolutionary Service:—A navy emblem on monument suggests service in the navy. The inscription is "A Revolutionary Soldier". Name recorded, 1909 by Miss E. L. Newhall, Sturgis. Data recorded, 1915, by Dr. Blanche M. Haines, Three Rivers, Mich.

BENJAMIN BULSON

BULSON, Benjamin, (alias Smith). Born 1754. Revolutionary Service:—Benj. Bulson enlisted, March, 1776, in N. Y.; company commanded by Capt. Thos. Mitchell, under Col. Van Courtlandt, in Gen. Putnam's brigade. He was captured by the British and sent to Halifax—escaped and re-enlisted. Served on board the "Junius Brutus" (also given "Julius Brutus") under Capt. John Brooks, which on its first cruise was captured by a British boat and to which Bulson was transferred as one of prize crew. Recaptured by the "Hornet", Bulson was sent aboard the old prison ship "Jersey", at Waalabout and sentenced to nine hundred lashes, for trying to escape; four hundred and fifty of which were given. He finally escaped in 1781. On prison ship he changed his name to Benj. Smith to avoid capture by Tory relatives. Filed declaration for pension July 21, 1823 at which time he was sixty-nine years old.

Authorities quoted:—*Oakland County History; Mich. Hist. Colls.*

Data recorded by Mrs. Lillian Drake Avery, Pontiac, Mich.

ELIAS CADY

CADY, Elias. Born at Providence, R. I., Sept. 7, 1756. Died March 31, 1853; buried in Oak Hill cemetery, Holly Twp., Oakland Co., Mich.; grave marked, Sept. 25, 1914, by General Richardson chapter, Pontiac.

Married Olive Baker of Providence, R. I., who died at Utica, N. Y., 1838.

Children:—Seth B.; Rhoda; Mary; Sarah; Philinda; and Elias.

Elias Cady, (Sr.) was the son of Benajar Cady.

Residences:—Providence, R. I.; Utica, N. Y.; Holly, Mich.

Revolutionary Service:—Enlisted at Boston during the first year of the war and served till the close. "He spent the winter in Valley Forge with Gen. Washington."

Came to Michigan, 1838; lived with son Seth B. at Holly, Michigan. He was a pensioner.

Authorities quoted:—*History of Oakland County*, I, 87–88; *Mich. Hist. Colls.*, XXXIX, 451.

Data recorded by Mrs. Lillian Drake Avery, Pontiac.

CALEB CARR, SR.

CARR, Caleb. Born Oct. 13, 1762.
Died July 18, 1839; buried in Novi cemetery; grave
marked, Oct. 3, 1914, by General Richardson chapter,
Pontiac.
Children:—Caleb, Jr., b. in Vermont (See note;) Isaac,
b. Sept. 6, 1790, Vt., d. Dec., 1862, m. at Redford,
Mich.; Calvin, b. Vt. and d. Waterford, Mich.;
Sarah, b. June 5, 1800; d. Feb. 9, 1837.
Occupation:—Methodist exhorter.
Revolutionary Service:—Enlisted Nov. 2, 1776; served
through an Indian alarm; was a private in Capt.
Millard's company, under Col. John Waterman; cor-
poral in Capt. Millard's company, 1st division, under
Col. Wakeman.
Came to Michigan:—The land records show that the
Carr family bought land in Kensington in the year
1836, at which time Caleb Carr, Jr., was a resident
of the place. A few years later the father and sons
lived at Novi, where Isaac Carr kept tavern, which
was burned in 1847.
Authorities quoted:—*Mass. Soldiers and Sailors*, III,
130; *History of Oakland County*, I, 89; *Mich. Hist.
Colls.*, XVIII, 449-451.
Ed. note:—Caleb Carr, Jr., is also buried in Novi
cemetery. In 1839, he was postmaster, inspector
of elections, supervisor, and justice of the peace;
1840, performed the first marriage in the township;
1842, built the first frame house in the township, a
16 by 24 and one and one-half stories high, which
was used as the first hotel. He ran the first blacksmith shop, had first wheat and corn ground at the
first mill in the township—The Red Cedar Mill;

1842, was re-elected postmaster. See *Mich. Hist. Colls.*, XVIII, 449, 452.

JOSHUA CHAMBERLAIN

CHAMBERLAIN, Joshua. Born, 1760.
Died Feb. 20, 1827; buried Oak Hill cemetery, Pontiac; grave marked, July 29, 1909, by the General Richardson chapter, Pontiac.
Married Sarah ———— who died, Aug. 14, 1814, at Gorham, N. Y.
Children:—Joshua, Jr.; Olmstead (Dr.).
Places of residence:—Lewiston, Niagara Co., N. Y.
Revolutionary Service:—Enlisted, April 3, 1777, at Richmond, Berkshire Co., Mass.; served as private until April 3, 1780, in Capt. Jeremiah Miller's company, Col. Vose regiment of Mass. troops.
Came to Michigan about 1820; located at Detroit and later lived with his sons in Pontiac.
Authorities quoted:—*Mich. Hist. Colls.*, XII, 579.; *History of Oakland County.*
Ed. note:—See also Pensioners of Territorial Michigan.

EZRA CHILSON

CHILSON, Ezra. Born at Scituate, R. I., Nov. 20, 1762.
Died Sept. 18, 1838; buried at Silver Brook, Niles, Mich.; grave marked, July 16, 1915, by Fort St. Joseph chapter, Niles.
Married Pamelia Dagget.
Children:— ———— b. Apr., 1793, d. May 3, 1793; Charlotte, b. Apr. 2, 1794; ————gham, b. Jan., 1797; Mandala; Charles; Caroline; Laura; Olive J.

Places of residence:—In 1778, Worthington, Mass.;
1780, Lanesborough, Mass.; 1782, Providence, R. I.;
Vergenes, Addison Co., Vt.
Revolutionary Service:—June or July, 1778 to Jan.,
1779, a private under Lt. Ingalls and Col. Sprout,
Mass. militia; 1782 two months service Hopkins
privateer, R. I.
Data recorded by Mrs. Grace Studley Smith, Niles.
Mich.

JEREMIAH CLARK

CLARK (also Clarke), Jeremiah. Born at Preston,
Conn., 1760 or '61.
Died, June 1, 1845; buried at Clarkston, Oakland Co.,
Mich.; grave marked, Sept. 17, 1908, by General
Richardson chapter, Pontiac.
Son of Jeremiah Clark (Clarke).[3]
Married Sarah Millington, 1780; b. 1767; d. July 17,
1845.
Children:—Julia; Amasa; Lydia, b. 1781, d. 1845;
Henry; Amos; Jeremiah, b. 1790, d. 1847; Lucy;
Amy, b. 1794, d. 1853; Susan, b. 1797; Hiram; Sarah,
b. 1806, d. 1872; Nelson, b. 1808, d. 1876; Sidney;
Ebenezer, b. 1812, d. 1868.
Places of residence:—Shaftsbury, Vt.; Bath, N. J.;
Nelson, N. Y.; Onondaga Co., N. Y.; Clarkston, Mich.
Revolutionary Service:—Served under Capt. Bigelow
Lawrence, entering service, March 2, 1778; dis-
charged May 2, 1778. The Vermont revolutionary
rolls record the name of Jeremiah Clark on the pay-

---

3. Jeremiah Clarke, Sr., was a major in 1777; member of first Council of
Safety of Vermont; Judge of the first court. Vermont Hist.
Society Pub. I, pp. 11, 15, 21, 23, 25; Vermont State Papers, pp
257, 266, 277, 553, 555.

roll of Capt. Samuel Robertson, under Lt. Col. Eben Walbridge, June 15 to July 10, 1778.

Came to Michigan; located in Clarkston, Oakland Co.

Authorities quoted:—*History of Oakland County*, I, 84; *Vt. Rev. Rolls*, 76; *Mich. Hist. Colls.*, XXXIX, 448.

Data recorded by Mrs. Lillian Drake Avery, Pontiac, Mich.

MOSES CLARK

CLARK, Moses. Born at Lebanon, Conn., Sept. 24, 1761.

Died at Alpine, Mich., Jan. 2, 1844; buried, Walker cemetery, Walker Twp., Kent Co.; grave marked, May 29, 1906, by Sophie de Marsac Campau chapter, Grand Rapids, Mich.

Married Patty Bill, who was born, Jan. 10, 1765, at Lebanon, Conn.; died at Alpine, Mich., Nov. 21, 1846.

Children:—Betsey, b. Sept., 1806 at Randon, N. C.; Charlie; Patty; Sophie; Erastus, b. Nov. 18, 1803, d. Feb. 4, 1880.

Revolutionary Service:—Enlisted, May, 1777, at the age of sixteen, at Lebanon, Conn.; a fifer for three years under Capt. John Hart and Col. Wm. Livingston; discharged May 31, 1780, at Morristown, N. Y.

At the age of seventy-two applied for a pension.

Came to Michigan, 1842; lived with son Erastus Clark.

Occupation:—Farmer.

Data recorded by Mrs. Herbery Morrill, Grand Rapids, Mich.

ELIJAH COOK

COOK, Elijah. Born, Sept. 10, 1759.

Died June 30, 1839; buried, Cook's Prairie cemetery, near Homer, Mich.; grave marked, June 17, 1916, by Charity Cook chapter, Homer.

Son of Jared and Ruth (Hutchinson) Cook; Jared was
born 1720.
Married Charity Lockwood who was born May 21,
1762 and d. Mar. 9, 1843. She was the dau. of
Joseph and Charity (Knapp) Lockwood.
Children of Elijah:—Sally, b. 1784; Betsey, b. 1787;
Ephiriam, b. 1787; Charity, b. 1789; Sabrina, b.
1791; Elijah, b. 1793; Elisha, b. 1795; a son, b. 1797;
Joseph, b. 1798; Jared, b. 1799; Sabrina (?), b.
1801; Nancy, b. 1803; Lydia, b. 1806.
Places of residence:—Conn.; Stephenson, N. Y.; Veron-
ica, N. Y.; Clarkston, N. Y.; Homer, Mich.
Revolutionary Service:—Enlisted, Jan., 1777, at Pres-
ton, Conn., under Capt. Nathaniel Webb, Lemuel
Clift and Phillips and Col. John Durkey. Was at
Valley Forge and at the battle of Monmouth, N. J.,
1778; Stony Point, N. Y., July 16, 1779.
Came to Michigan in 1836; located three miles west of
Homer and lived with his son Elijah.
Data recorded by Mrs. William H. Cortright, Homer,
Mich.

JOHN CRAWFORD

CRAWFORD, John.
Buried in Meade cemetery; grave marked by Alexander
Macomb chapter, Mt. Clemens, Oct., 1914.
Revolutionary Service:—Served in the Revolution; was
a lieutenant in the levies of 1791; a captain in the
infantry, 1792; in fourth sublegion, 1792; honorably
discharged, Nov. 1, 1796; served in the war of 1812.
Authorities quoted:—Gen. Wayne's *Orderly Book;*
Mich. Hist. Colls., XXXIV, 482.
Data filed by Alexander Macomb chapter, Mt.
Clemens, Mich.

Ed. note:—In General Wayne's *Orderly Book*, a John Crauford is given as a member of the 2nd battalion of infantry, under Major Ballard Smith, and Crauford as commandant of Fort Fayette.

EBENEZER CROMBIE

CROMBIE, Ebenezer.
Grave located by Sarah Caswell Angell chapter, Ann Arbor, Mich.
Revolutionary Service:—Served as a sergeant in the Revolutionary war.
Record placed on file by the Sarah Caswell Angell chapter, Ann Arbor.

JEDUTHAN CROSS

CROSS, Jeduthan. Born Oct. 15, 1764.
Died at Adrian, 1839; buried at Oakwood; grave marked May 25, 1911, by the Lucy Wolcott Barnum Chapter, Adrian, Mich.
Son of Abel Cross.
Married twice. Second wife Mehitabel Ellis, who died at Adrian, 1837.
Revolutionary Service:—Served through the war.
Came to Michigan, 1836; located at Adrian.
Data recorded by Lucy Wolcott Barnum chapter, Adrian, Mich.

JOSIAH CROSSMAN

CROSSMAN, Josiah. Born at Norton, Mass., Nov. 25, 1760.
Buried in the Davis cemetery; grave marked, May 14, 1904, by the Alexander Macomb chapter, Mt. Clemens, Mich.

Josiah was the son of Elkanah Crossman who served in the Revolution.

Children:—There were fourteen children; Timothy E., the only one recorded (1918).

Places of Residence:—Norton, Mass.; Victor, Ontario Co., N. Y.; Washington, Macomb Co., (1849).

Revolutionary Service:—Enlisted Jan. 1, 1776; served thirteen and one-half months as a private under Capt. James Perry and Col. Paul D. Sargeant, in Mass. militia; for six months as private under Silas Cobb and Col. Danforth Keves, in Mass.; March 16, 1778, one year as 4th sergeant under Capt. Philip Traffam and Col. John Topham, in R. I. Was in battles of White Plains, N. Y., Oct. 28, 1776, and Trenton, N. J.

Authorities quoted:—Bureau of Pensions.

Data recorded by Agnes L. Snover, Mt. Clemens, Mich.

TIMOTHY CRUTTENDEN

CRUTTENDEN (Crittenden), Timothy.   Born about 1746.

Died 1842 (?); buried in Oakhill cemetery near Saline, Mich.

Grave marked, July 10, 1913, (though its exact location not determined), by Ypsilanti chapter.

Children:—Hannah; Jarius, 1774–1843; Roda; Julius; ——— a dau.; Pauline.

Timothy Cruttenden was the son of Hull Cruttenden.

Revolutionary Service:—Timothy with his brother Stephen went down Lake Champlain on the ice, against a strong wind, to look out a camping ground in the lee of some hill on shore that the little band

of patriots might be somewhat protected from the
northern blasts. They were at the time on the
march to the siege of Quebec. Family history of the
Cruttendens quoted in a letter written by H. A.
Hodge, Ann Arbor, 1918.
Data recorded by Ypsilanti chapter, Ypsilanti, Mich.,
and H. A. Hodge, Ann Arbor.
Ed. note:—A family history of the Cruttendens was
compiled by Dr. Albert Crittenden, Clifton Springs,
N. Y.

JOSIAH CUTLER

CUTLER, Josiah.
Buried in Forest Hill cemetery, Ann Arbor, Mich.;
grave marked, 1909, by Sarah Caswell Angell chapter,
Ann Arbor.
Served through the Revolution.
Data recorded by the Sarah Caswell Angell chapter.

JOSEPH DARLING

DARLING, Joseph.   Born at Middleborough, Mass.,
Sept. 3, 1764.
Died June 3, 1844; buried at Jackson; grave marked,
July 10, 1918, by Algonquin chapter of St. Joseph
and Benton Harbor and the Sarah Treat Prudden
chapter of Jackson, Mich.
Descendants of Joseph Darling:—A son named Chris-
topher Columbus, born July 10, 1800, died May 20,
1880. The children of Columbus were Hulda; John
G.; Theodore; Frances M.; Sarah; and Henry Clay.
Among the living relatives, 1918, were Mrs. W. H.
Reitzt; Mrs. James Jakway; Mrs. Closson; Miss
Kathleen Johnson; Miss Beatrice Jakway of Benton
Harbor, members of Algonquin chapter.

Places of residence:—Boston, Mass.; Woodstock, Vt.; Coldsprings, N. Y. and Jackson, Mich.
Revolutionary Service from 1780 through the war.
Came to Michigan, 1832, with his father and brother; located on N. W. ¼, S. 35, T. 2, S. R. 11 W.
Authorities quoted:—*Mich Hist. Colls.*
Data recorded by Mrs. H. S. Gray, Benton Harbor, Mich.
Ed. note.—"Joseph Darling enlisted at the age of sixteen as a substitute for his father". See also Pensioners of Territorial Michigan.

FRANCIS DELONG

DeLong, Francis. Born 1760.
Died Feb. 8, 1862; buried in Hartford cemetery, Van Buren Co.; grave marked, June 10, 1915, by Algonquin chapter, St. Joseph and Benton Harbor, Mich.
Children:—Eight. Living relatives, 1917:—Silas DeLong, Bangor, Mich.; Mrs. Lewis Landon, Hartford, Mich.
Revolutionary Service:—"Enlisted Sept. 13, 1777."
Came to Michigan, 1854; located in Hartford Twp., Van Buren Co.
Data recorded by Mrs. Grace V. Canaran and Mrs. H. S. Gray of the Algonquin chapter.

ALTAMONT DONALDSON

Donaldson, Altamont. Born Nov. 13, 1763.
Died Jan. 26, 1847; buried at Fenton; grave marked by Genesee chapter, of Flint, Mich., Sept. 20, 1915.[6]

---

6. In a letter Nov., 1918, to Dr. Haines, State Chairman of Preservation of Historic Spots Committee, Mrs. G. E. Pomeroy, of Flint, records the marking of the grave as occurring in June, 1915.

Revolutionary Service:—Served through the war.
Data recorded by Genesee chapter.

ELIJAH DRAKE

DRAKE, Elijah.   Born near the Delaware Water Gap,
  Northampton Co., Pa., July 4, 1759.
Died April 8, 1848; buried at Royal Oak, Mich.; grave
  marked, July 10, 1900, by the General Richardson
  chapter, Pontiac, Mich.
Son of Samuel Drake.
Elijah D. married Abigal Stoddard, 1790, at Newton
  Point.   Abigal was the dau. of Thos. Stoddard.   She
  died Feb. 20, 1860.
Children of Elijah D.:— Sally, b. Jan. 11, 1791;
  Wealthy, b. Mar. 4, 1793; Samuel, b. Aug. 27, 1795;
  Thomas Jefferson, b. Apr. 18, 1797; Cyrus, b. Dec.
  24, 1800; Elias, b. Sept. 25, 1803; Elijah, b. Dec. 24,
  1805; Flemon, b. Apr. 30, 1807; Edward L., b. Apr.
  30, 1810; Morgan, b. Oct. 18, 1813.
Places of residence:—Delaware Water Gap; North-
  umberland Co., Pa.; Chemung, N. Y.; Scipio, N. Y.;
  Genesee Co., N. Y.; Oakland Co., Mich.; Ann Arbor,
  Mich.; Royal Oak, Mich.
Revolutionary Service:—An associator, May 22, 1775,
  Northampton Co., Pa., militia; a lieutenant under
  Jacob Stroud; a captain, 1776; in 1778, under
  Capt. Schoonhoven; 1799, under Col. Armstrong,
  Northampton Co., Pa.
Came to Michigan, 1835; located in Oakland Co.,
  with five sons and their families.   The second son,
  Thomas J., located in Oakland Co., in 1824.
Authorities quoted:—*History of Oakland County*, I, 82;
  Pa. Archives, 2nd Series, XIV, 555, 576.

Data recorded by Mrs. Lillian Drake Avery, Pontiac, Mich.

Ed. note:—In the *Mich. Hist. Colls.* XXXIX, 445, the pension records are quoted as 'Mrs. Avery's authority for the following:—"Elijah Drake enlisted as a private and served six months under Capt. Benj. Schoonhover, Colonel Stroud's regiment, Pennsylvania; he re-enlisted June 5, 1779, for three months under the same captain in Colonel Armstrong's regiment, Pennsylvania. He later served fifteen days under Capt. Samuel Shoemaker. His place of residence was given as Lower Smithville, Northampton County, Pennsylvania."

CONRAD DUBOIS

DuBois, Conrad.

Revolutionary Service:—Conrad DuBois served in Captain Hasbrouck's company, Col. John Cantine's regiment, N. Y. troops in 1778.

Name recorded by Lansing chapter, Lansing.

See also Martin DuBois.

MARTIN DUBOIS

DuBois, Martin. Born at New Platz, N. Y., Oct. 21, 1764.

Died 1854; buried in Fitchburg cemetery, Leslie, Mich.; grave located by Elijah Grout chapter of Leslie.

The Martin DuBois line "traces descent from Geoffroi du Bois, a companion and friend of Duke William. Martin was the son of Conrad DuBois."

Martin DuBois married Margerite Avery who died on the same day her husband died and both buried in same grave.

Revolutionary Service:—"Martin DuBois was a bugler,
and the conch shell which he used for a bugle is in
the possession of his grand-daughter, Mrs. Julia
DuBois Price, a resident of Lansing, (1917)."
Came to Michigan in his ninetieth year; located in
Bunkerhill Twp., Ingham Co.; lived with son.
Ed. note:— *New York in Rev.* gives Martin DuBois as
a private in Col. Wessenfel's regiment, Ulster Co.,
N. Y., levies, 1777. Conrad DuBois, the father of
Martin, served in Capt. Hasbrouck's company, Col.
John Cantine's regiment, N. Y. troops, in 1778.
Name recorded by Lansing chapter, Lansing. See
also Pensioners of Territorial Michigan.
Data recorded by Mrs. Franc Adams, Leslie, Mich.

SAMUEL DUNN

Dunn, Samuel.
Buried at Plymouth, Wayne Co., Mich.; grave marked
by the Louisa St. Clair chapter, Detroit.
Places of residence:—Newton, N. J.; Wayne Co., Mich.
Revolutionary Service:—Enlisted, Dec., 1775, under
Col. Maxwell in N. J. militia; 1776, for six months
under Col. Butler; 1778, for nine months in Capt.
Spaulding's co., Conn. militia. Was in massacre
of Wyoming, Pa., 1778. Application for pension,
Oct. 2, 1832.
Data recorded by Miss Gracie Brainerd Krum, his-
torian of Louisa St. Clair chapter, Detroit.

RUFUS EARLE

Earle, Rufus.
Buried in Barren Lake cemetery, near Niles, Cass Co.,
Mich.; grave marked, Oct. 2, 1915, by Algonquin
chapter, St. Joseph and Benton Harbor.

Living descendants (1917):—Alice E. Atwood, Cassopolis, Mich.; Albert E. Earl, South Bend, Ind.
Residence:—"Lived at one time in New York."
Revolutionary Service:—Served as private through the war.
Came to Michigan, 1835, where he took up a large tract of land near Niles.
Data recorded by Mrs. H. S. Gray of the Algonquin chapter.

JAMES EMMONS

EMMONS, James. Born in Frederickstown, Va., 1760.
Died 1839; buried, Riverside cemetery, Dowagiac, Mich.; grave marked, June 25, 1915, by Algonquin chapter, St. Joseph and Benton Harbor.
Places of residence:—In the states of North Carolina, Virginia, and in Cass Co., Mich.
Came to Michigan, 1834; located in Cass Co.; lived with youngest son, John E. Emmons.
Living relative recorded, 1918, Mrs. John Tichnor, Dowagiac, Mich.

EDWARD EVANS

EVANS, Edward. Born May 8, 1766.
Died Dec. 27, 1853; buried at Constantine, Mich.; grave located, 1907, by the Abiel Fellows chapter, Three Rivers; marked, Sept., 1917, by Algonquin chapter, St. Joseph and Benton Harbor.
Grandchildren:—Alonzo; Zilba; Franklin; Mary (?); Amelia.
The following is quoted from the obituary, appearing in the Constantine *Mercury*, Jan. 17, 1854:—"His

youth was spent amidst the stirring events of our revolution. He entered the Revolutionary army in 1781 at the age of fifteen; was employed for two years in active service. He was honorably discharged with his compatriots at the city of Albany—independence being achieved.

"He soon after enlisted for another warfare from which there is no discharge. He entered the ministry in 1789. His first settlement was in the town of Enfield, Grafton Co., N. H. He labored with great success. His character and talents were so highly esteemed, in this part of the country, that the people selected him four years to come as their representative in the Legislature. After he retired from the Legislature he received the appointment of Judge of Probate for the same county. He continued to fill this office for a period of 12 years.

"At this period of his life, he was led to turn his face to what was then the great migration to the West, emigration towards Western N. Y. and Ohio. The last seven years of his life was spent with his children. He removed four years ago to our village for the purpose of enjoying the public sanctuary. He will be missed from the pulpit, for there he was always found. But none will miss him more than the ministry of our village.

"The following resolutions were adopted by the Siloam Lodge of Free and Accepted Masons in this village.

"RESOLVED. That in the death of the Rev. Edward Evans this Lodge sustains a peculiarly heavy bereavement.

Submitted by C. S. Engle, W. M.

J. R. Price, Sect'y."

Copied by Mrs. Carrie V. Davis, Constantine, Mich.
Living descendants:—Ziba Evans, grandson; Ansel
Evans, great-grandson; Bertha Mabel Evans, Lin-
den, S. D., great-granddaughter.
Data recorded by Mrs. H. P. Barrows in *National
Magazine*, 1914, and Dr. Blanche M. Haines, Three
Rivers, Mich., (1915), in the chapter records.

ABIEL FELLOWS

FELLOWS, Abiel. Born at Caanan, Conn., Oct. 17,
1764.
Died 1833; buried on the Fellows farm near School-
craft; grave marked, July 25, 1908, by Abiel Fellows
chapter, Three Rivers, Mich.
Son of Abiel and Elizabeth (Roe) Fellows, married
Jan., 1758. Abiel Fellows, Sr., was born Oct. 29,
1734, was the son of Ephraim, the son of William.
Married:—1st.—Anna Andrus (Andress), b. Apr. 17,
1767; m. Nov. 12, 1786; d. Jan. 23, 1789. 2nd.—
Catherine Mann, b. 1773; m. Feb. 17, 1791; d. Aug.
17, 1803. 3rd.—Dorcas Hopkins, b. 1786.
Children by second wife:—Andress, Amanda, Ann,
Almira, Abiel, Asahel; third wife:—Katherine, Thos.
J., James M., Simon S., Timothy H., John M., Caro-
line, Emma, Sarah, Orville, Milo, Elizabeth, Lucy.
Places of residence:—Luzern Co., Pa.; Schoolcraft,
Kalamazoo Co., Mich.
Revolutionary Service:—In battle of Freeman's farm,
N. Y., Sept. 19, 1777; and at Saratoga, 1777.
Came to Michigan, 1829; located on farm near School-
craft, Kalamazoo Co. "Was first postmaster in
Kalamazoo Co., and assessed the first tax levied on
that county."

Authorities quoted:—Family records.

Data recorded by Miss Anna Fellows, Schoolcraft, Mich., and Mrs. Wilbur Hackett, Three Rivers.

Ed. note:—The following descendants of Abiel Fellows are or have been members of the Three Rivers chapter, Daughters of the American Revolution, named in his honor the "Abiel Fellows" chapter:— Mrs. Lucy (Fellows) Andrews, organizing regent; Mrs. Maude (Fellows) Aspinwall; Mrs. Gertrude (Knowles) Chamberlain; Mrs. William T. Callender; Mrs. Milissa L. Carver; Miss D. F. Carpenter; Mrs. Kate (Fellows) Dean; Mrs. Ella H. Dolloff; Mrs. Mary H. Duncan; Miss Anna Fellows; Mrs. Alice Hackett; Mrs. Anna Sadie (Fellows) Hackett; Mrs. John Hrdlicka; Mrs. Harriet (Fellows) Ikler; Mrs. Charlotte W. K. Kellam; Mrs. Almira Kellogg; Mrs. Maude L. Simonds; Miss Florence A. Chapin.

BENJAMIN FERRIS

Ferris, Benjamin.

Died at the age of one hundred; buried on the farm of his grandson near Athens, Calhoun Co., Mich. Name officially recorded by Abiel Fellows chapter, Three Rivers, Mich.

Places of Residence:—In the state of Conn.; Sherburn, Chenango Co., N. Y.; Athens, Mich.

Revolutionary Service:—Served as captain in the war.

Came to Mich., in the spring of 1832; located at Athens, Calhoun Co. "Mr. & Mrs. Ferris lived with their grandson, Benj. Ferris."

Data recorded by Mrs. George Nicholls, Leonidas.

BENJAMIN GRACE

GRACE, Benjamin. Born 1760.
Died on Wm. Grace farm, Nov. 15, 1851; buried in the
Clarenceville cemetery; grave marked, Aug. 3, 1910,
by General Richardson chapter, Pontiac, Mich.
Children:—Benjamin; Mary; James B., b. Apr. 27,
1789; Hannah, b. June 13, 1791; William; Abigail;
Amasa, b. Aug., 1797; Sally, b. 1802; Amelia; Har-
riet, b. Mar. 17, 1807; Darius, b. Oct. 8, 1809,
Revolutionary Service:—Private in N. H. militia,
Enlisted at Amherst, N. H., 1780, served under
Capt. Livermore and Col, Scammel until 1783,
Came to Michigan, 1828; resided with his children at
Farmington, Oakland Co.
Authorities:—Pension records; *Mich, Hist, Colls.; His-
tory of Oakland Co,*
Data recorded by Mrs. Lillian Drake Avery, Pontiac.
Ed, note.—See also Pensioners of Territorial Michigan.

JAMES GRAHAM

GRAHAM (Grimes), James. Born 1749.
Died Sept. 5, 1837; buried in Graham family cemetery,
Avon; grave marked, June 2, 1911, by General Rich-
ardson chapter, Pontiac.
Married Mary Van de Mark, (a native of Holland);
she died Sept. 7, 1835.
Children:—James; David; John; Alexander; Williams;
Benjamin, b. 1808, d. 1864; Chester; Martha; Mary.
Places of residence:—New York City; Tioga Point, Pa.;
Canada; 1816 at Mt. Clemens, Mich.; later Oakland
Co., Mich,

Revolutionary Service:—Enlisted Apr. 15, 1777 in Capt. Hewitt's co., Col. Dennison's regiment, Conn. militia. In Capt. Spaulding's company, Col. Butler's regiment.

Came to Michigan, 1816; was first white settler of Oakland Co. Tradition claims that in his eagerness to come to America, James Graham became an indentured servant to a New York physician.

Authorities quoted:—*History of Oakland County*, Vol. I, ch. 6; *Mich. Hist. Colls.*

Data recorded by Mrs. Lillian Drake Avery, Pontiac.

DR. ISAAC GRANT

GRANT, Isaac. Born 1759.

Died Nov. 9, 1841; buried at Albion; grave marked, June 17, 1906, by Hannah Tracy Grant chapter, Albion.

Married Hannah Tracy, who died Oct. 30, 1841, aged seventy-six years.

Children:—Charles, b. Colrain, Mass., Oct. 2, 1794, d. on farm in Bengal, Jan. 11, 1885.

Places of residence:—Whitingham, Vt.; Chenango Co., N. Y.

Revolutionary Service:—Enlisted when fifteen and served through six campaigns; a prisoner of war on the old "Jersey" prison ship; exchanged; was at Valley Forge; acted as an orderly for "Mad Anthony Wayne."

Occupation:—Physician.

Came to Michigan; lived with his son Charles at Albion.

Authorities quoted:—*Mich. Hist. Colls.*, VIII, 26-27.

Data recorded by Hannah Tracy Grant chapter, Albion.

GREEN, Levi. Born at Coventry, R. I., June 6, 1758.
Died, West Bloomfield, Oakland Co., June 21, 1859;
buried North Farmington cemetery; grave marked,
June 14, 1906, by General Richardson chapter, Pon-
tiac, Mich.
Married Asenath Robinson.
Children:—Aurelia, b. Nov. 5, 1778; Eunice; Water-
mann; Sophia; Fanny, b. Apr. 3, 1794; Horace;
Hulda, b. Sept. 24, 1799; Zephaniah Ripley, b. Aug.
6, 1801; Emma, b. Apr. 24, 1804; Speedy, b. May
25, 1808; Laura, b. Aug. 11, 1811.
Places of residence:—Livonia, N. Y.; West Bloomfield.
Revolutionary Service:—Enlisted, July 1, 1776, for
eight months under Capt. Baldwin. Second enlist-
ment was for month of July, 1777, under Capt.
Newell. His third enlistment was Aug., 1777, under
Capt. Brown, Col. Simond's regiment, Mass. militia.
Was in battle of Bennington, Vt., Aug. 16, 1777.
His grandson, Mr. Horace A. Green, has in his pos-
session the original pension papers, and powder horn
carved with his name which was carried through the
war.
Came to Michigan to live with his son Zephaniah Ripley
Green, who came to West Bloomfield, July, 1832.
Authorities quoted:—*History of Oakland County*, Vol. I,
ch. 6.
Data recorded by Mrs. Lillian Drake Avery, Pontiac.

GREGORY, Esbon.
Buried in the Pains cemetery, one and one-quarter
miles east of Troy Corners, Oakland Co., Mich,

Married Salome Sherwood.

Children:—Solomon; Abigail; Salome; Mary Ann; Jesse, b. 1769.

Places of residence:—1777, New Ashford or Lanesborough, N. Y.; 1818, Manilius, N. Y.; 1833, Hanover, N. Y.; 1837, Troy, Oakland Co., Mich.

Revolutionary Service:—Esbon Gregory enlisted June 15, 1777, and served till Aug. 17, 1777, as private in Capt. Amariah Babbitt's company, Col. Benj. Simon's regiment, Mass. militia. Re-enlisted Aug. 17, 1777, served till Oct. 17, 1777, under Capt. Herrick and Col. Seth Warner. From Oct. 17, 1777, to May or June, 1778 as a teamster under Capt. Luther Loomis and Col. Warner. 1778, for eight months in Capt. Peter Porter's company, Gen. Stark's life guard; 1779, for three months as quartermaster, for Gen. Stark; also served as sergeant under Capt. Barnes in Col. Israel Capen's regiment; 1780–1781, he served as sergeant under Captains Hickok, Spoor and Gross and Colonels Brown and Willett. Was in battles of Bennington, Vt., Aug. 16, 1777; Stone Arabia, N. Y., Oct. 19, 1780; Johnstown, N. Y.

Authorities quoted:—Pension Bureau, Washington; *History of Oakland County*, Vol. I, ch. 6.

Data recorded by Mrs. Lillian Drake Avery, Pontiac.

SOUTHMAYD GUERNSEY

GUERNSEY, Southmayd. Born at Watertown, Conn., Apr. 10, 1763.

Died Apr. 4, 1850; buried at Athens, Mich.; grave marked, May 13, 1916, by Battle Creek chapter, Battle Creek, Mich.

Married Sabra Scott, b. Jan. 14, 1766; d. July 12, 1836.

Children:—Raphael;   Laura;   Rebecca;   Jonothan;
    Amanda.
Revolutionary Service:—Enlisted in Conn. militia;
    served at the age of thirteen and received honorable
    discharge.
Data recorded by Battle Creek chapter, Battle Creek,
    Mich.

WILLIAM HALLOCK

HALLOCK, William. Major.
Buried on Kalmback farm, Washtenaw Co.; grave
    located by Sarah Caswell Angell chapter, Ann Arbor,
    Mich.
Name recorded by Mrs. William H. Wait, Ann Arbor,
    Mich.

JOHN FRANCIS HAMTRAMCK

HAMTRAMCK, John Francis.   Born in Canada, 1757.
Died April 11, 1803; buried in Elliot lot, Mt. Elliot,
    Detroit, Mich.; grave marked, June 14, 1916, by
    Louisa St. Clair chapter, Detroit, Mich. "A monu-
    ment was erected to his honor by the officers whom he
    commanded."
Married:—Rebecca ————.
Children:—John Francis, b. 1798, at Ft. Wayne, Ind.;
    d. Apr. 21, 1858 at Sheperdston, Vt. John F. was a
    colonel in the Mexican war and in 1848, governor of
    Saltillo. The following is quoted from *Historical
    Register*, p. 496. "Ind. sergt. 1st inf. in 1813 and
    '14; cadet M. A. 26th Sept., 1815; 2nd lt. corps art.
    1st July, 1819; tr. to 3rd art. 1st June, 1821; res'd 1st
    Mar. 1822; col. 1st Va. vols. 31st Dec., 1846; hon.
    mustered out 20th June, 1848. (Died 21st Apr.,
    1858)."

Places of residence:—Northern N. Y.; Fort Wayne,
Ind.; Detroit, Mich.
Revolutionary Service:—"Capt. in Dubois, N. Y. reg.
in Revolution; maj. of inf. Sept. 29, 1789; lt. col.
commanding 1st sublegion, Feb., 1793. Commanded left wing of Gen. Wayne's army at Miami,
1794. Commandant, 1793. Personally thanked by
Washington." The *Historical Register* gives Col.
Hamtramck's service as follows: "Capt. 5th N. Y.,
21st Nov., 1776; tr. to 2nd N. Y., 1st Jan., 1783,
and served to 3rd June, 1783; capt. U. S. inf. regt.
12th Apr., 1785; maj. 20th Oct., 1786; maj. 1st
inf. U. S. A. 29th Sept., 1789; assigned to 2nd sublegion 4th Sept., 1792; lt. col. commandant 1st
sublegion 18th Feb., 1793; assigned to 1st U. S. inf.
1st Nov., 1796; col. 1st Apr., 1802; died Apr., 1803."
Gen. Wayne's *Orderly Book* records that "Col. Hamtramck was in command of advance guard of Wayne's
army at Detroit which evacuated, July 11, 1796;
possession taken July 13, 1796."
Located at Detroit:—1st U. S. commandant of Detroit
and its dependencies.
Data filed by Miss Gracie B. Krum, Detroit, Mich.
Ed. note:—*Mich. Hist. Colls.*, XIII, gives date of birth
Aug. 14, 1754; monument gives age 48 yrs., 7 mo.,
28 da. and death occurring Apr. 11, 1803.

JAMES HARRINGTON

HARRINGTON, James. Born 1763.
Died Oakland Co., 1825, aged sixty-two.
Married Martha Hould.
Daughter:—Mary, married Elias Gates.

Revolutionary Service:—Served in R. I. troops as a corporal.

Came to Michigan, 1820 or '21, located at West Bloomfield, May 15, 1823. Entered the entire section 36.

Authorities quoted:—*History of Oakland County*, Vol. I, ch. 6. *Mich. Hist. Colls.*, XXII.

Data recorded by Mrs. Lillian Drake Avery, Pontiac.

MASON HATFIELD

HATFIELD, Mason. "Deacon."

Buried at Stony Creek cemetery, near Saline, Mich.; grave marked, July 10, 1913, by Ypsilanti chapter, Ypsilanti, Mich.

Revolutionary Service:—Served through war.

Data recorded by Ypsilanti chapter.

ISAAC HICKMAN

HICKMAN, Isaac. Born at Great Egg Harbor, N. J., June 4, 1757.

Died, Aug. 15, 1845; buried at Oak Hill, Battle Creek, Mich.; grave marked, May 13, 1916, by Battle Creek chapter.

Married:—Second wife, Susannah Hunnon.

Children:—Geo. D. Hickman, b. Mar. 23, 1820; John E., b. 1822.

Living descendants:—(1917) Mrs. Julia Hickman and Miss Dorothy Squire, Battle Creek, Mich.

Data recorded by Battle Creek chapter, Battle Creek, Mich.

JOSEPH HOLLAND

HOLLAND, Joseph. Born at New London, Conn., Oct., 1760.

Buried at Romeo; grave marked, Oct., 1914, by Alexander Macomb chapter, Mt. Clemens, Mich.
Places of residence:—Bozrah, New London Co., Conn., at date of enlistment; Washington, Macomb Co., Mich., at date of pension.
Revolutionary Service:—Enlisted, Nov., 1775 for one year; Aug., 1777, for one month; Oct., 1778, for two months; was private under Col. Burrall; was in the siege of Quebec.
Authorities quoted:—Bureau of Pensions.
Data recorded by Miss Agnes Snover, Mt. Clemens, Mich.
Ed. note:—See also Pensioners of Territorial Michigan.

GEORGE HORTON

Horton, George. Born 1761.
Died 1835; last pension paid Mar. 4, 1835; buried at Rochester; grave marked, July 29, 1909, by General Richardson chapter, Pontiac.
Married:—Elsie ————; d. Feb., 1827; buried in Rochester cemetery.
Children:—Benjamin, who entered land in section 21.
Places of residence:—Northampton Co., Pa.; 1809, Port Colborne, Canada; 1820, Yarmouth, Ontario; 1825, Oakland Co., Mich.
Revolutionary Service:—Enlisted May, 1780, at the age of nineteen, in Capt. Shoemaker's Pa. troops; served until Sept., 1783; the *Pa. Archives*, fifth series, records his service in the second class, seventh company, fifth battalion, Pa. militia, for 1782.
Came to Michigan, settled in Avon Twp., two miles south of Rochester; lived with son-in-law, Cornelius Decker, on section 22.

Authorities quoted:—*History of Oakland County*, Vol. I, ch. 6.

Data recorded by Mrs. Lillian Drake Avery, Pontiac.

Ed. note:—See also Pensioners of Territorial Michigan.

ENOCH HOTCHKISS

HOTCHKISS, Enoch.
Buried in the orchard on his farm in Oakland Co., Mich.; name reported by General Richardson chapter, Pontiac.
Revolutionary service claimed.
Came to Michigan, 1819; located in Oakland Co., near Pontiac.
Occupation:—Farmer.
Authorities quoted:—*Mich. Hist. Colls.*, III, 561; *History of Oakland County*, Vol. I, ch. 6.

BROOKS HOWARD

HOWARD, Brooks, Born, Nova Scotia, Mar. 14, 1765.
Died July 5, 1858; buried Chesterfield cemetery; grave marked, 1912, by Alexander Macomb chapter, Mt. Clemens, Mich.
Son of John Howard.
Places of residence:—Brookfield, Mass.; Royalton, Vt.; Macomb Co., Mich.
Revolutionary Service:—Enlisted, Apr., 1781, at Royalton, Windsor Co., Vt.; served as a private under Capt. Benjamin and Col. Waite.
Came to Michigan, about 1835; lived in Macomb Co., Michigan, 1855, near "Territorial" road running through West Chesterfield and East Macomb.
Data recorded by Alexander Macomb chapter, Mt. Clemens.

ABRAHAM HUFF

HUFF, Abraham.   Born 1760.
Died 1850; buried in Shurte cemetery, LaGrange Twp.,
    Cass Co.; grave marked, Oct. 2, 1915, by Algonquin
    chapter, St. Joseph and Benton Harbor.
Data recorded by Mrs. H. S. Gray, Algonquin chapter,
    St. Joseph and Benton Harbor.

DERRICK HULICK

HULICK, Derrick.   Born Montgomery Twp., Somerset
    Co., N. J.
Died 1843.   The first person buried in Lakeville ceme-
    tery, Oakland Co.; grave marked, Sept. 16, 1916, by
    the General Richardson chapter, Pontiac.
Places of residence:—Somerset Co., N. J.; Oxford Twp.,
    Warren Co., N. J.; Addison Twp., Oakland Co.,
    Mich.
Revolutionary Service:—Enlisted, June 1, 1776, in
    Capt. Wm. Baird's company, under Col. Quick; also
    under Capt. Rynear Staats and Col. Frelinghuysen
    of N. J.; re-enlisted in 1777 for eight months in John
    Baird's company, Col. Webster's regiment; and in
    April, 1778, for two months under Capt. Joakim
    Gulick and John Blair in Col. Van Dyke's regiment.
    Feb., 1779, enlisted for six months and in 1780 for one
    month in same company.   Sept. 3, 1832, he applied
    for and was allowed a pension.   Said to have served
    in war of 1812.
Came to Michigan, 1839; lived with dau., Mrs. Dennis
    Snyder.
Authorities:—*History of Oakland County*, I, 91; *New
    Jersey in Revolution; Mich. Hist. Colls.*, XXXIX, 454.

AMOS INGRAM

INGRAM, Amos. Born in State of New York, 1757.
Died Aug. 11, 1838; buried at Irving, Hastings, Mich.;
grave marked by the Emily Virginia Mason chapter,
Hastings.
Son:—Frederick.
Grandchildren:—William W.; Velorus; Orril L.
Revolutionary Service: — Undoubtedly under Gen.
Washington, as he told of making forced marches of
seventy miles under Gen. Washington's command.
Came to Michigan in the spring of 1838; lived for a few
months on a farm with his son Frederick; died of
"chills and fever—the first white man to die in
Irving".
Data recorded by Mrs. Charles A. Weissert, Hastings.

SOLOMON JONES

JONES, Solomon. Born near Saybrook, Conn., 1760.
Died, "1865 at age of 105 years"; buried in Davisburg
cemetery; grave marked, July 6, 1916, by General
Richardson chapter, Pontiac, Mich.
Married:—(2nd) Mrs. Hannah Friday.
Children:—Polly; Chauncey; Daniel, came to Mich.,
from Orwell, Vt., in 1837; Isaac; Timothy, came to
Mich. in 1836, locat'd at Springfield; Wealthy, b.
1808, d. Aug. 14, 18 ., m. Silas Phillips, moved to
Mich., 1839; Jesse, b. in Essex Co., N. Y., came to
Mich., 1838, located at Groveland, Oakland Co.,
m. Charlotte Northrup.
Places of residence:—Saybrook, Conn.; state of Ver-
mont, Rutland Co.; Springfield, Mich.; and Grove-
land, Mich.

Revolutionary Service:—Enlisted, July, 1775, in Capt.
Abyah Rowle's 6th company, Conn. militia stationed
on the Sound until Sept. 14; ordered to Boston.
Came to Michigan, 1843; located at Springfield; lived
at Groveland five years with son Jesse.
Data recorded by Mrs. Lillian Drake Avery, Pontiac.
Ed. note:—Family tradition claims Solomon Jones
served through Revolutionary war and in war of 1812;
was in the 4th Vt. militia at Plattsburg, Sept,, 1814,

EBEN KIMBALL

KIMBALL, Eben.
Buried at Willow Grove, Armada; grave marked, Oct.,
1914, by Alexander Macomb chapter, Mt. Clemens,
Revolutionary Service:—Served through the Revolu-
tion; service not recorded.
Came to Michigan in 1829; purchased land in Washing-
ton Twp., Macomb Co. *Mich. Hist. Colls.*, XXVI, 549.
Data recorded by Alexander Macomb chapter, Mt.
Clemens.

NATHAN LANDON

LANDON, Nathan.   Born 1757.
Revolutionary Service:—Nathan Landon was the last
of the Revolutionary soldiers to file a declaration in
Oakland courts for a pension, which he did Nov. 13,
1828, at the age of seventy-one.   He enlisted Feb.
1, 1776, in Capt. Archibald Shaw's company, Col.
Wm. C. Maxwell's regiment, N. J. militia.   Served
until Nov. 14, 1776, when regiment was dismissed,
by Gen. Gates, at Ticonderoga.
Came to Michigan about 1828; lived with son Stephen
Landon, Oakland Co.
Data recorded by Mrs. Lillian Drake Avery, Pontiac,

LEVI LAWRENCE

LAWRENCE, Levi. Born Athol, Mass., Aug. 9, 17—.
Died Dec. 10, 1838, at Burford, Ont.; buried at Saginaw,
Mich.
Married:—Abigail Burdick Jones.
Living descendant:—Mrs. A. Spencer, Marlette, Mich.
Data under investigation by Saginaw chapter, Saginaw,
Mich.

ABIATHAR LINCOLN

LINCOLN, Abiathar.
Buried in Chapell cemetery, near Jackson; grave
marked, June 17, 1916, by Sarah Treat Prudden
chapter, Jackson, Mich.
Living descendants:—Mrs. Charles Pratt, Jackson;
Mrs. Henry B. Berger, Ann Arbor.
Data under investigation by Sarah Treat Prudden
chapter, Jackson.

HENRY LYBROOK

LYBROOK, Henry. Born 1755.
Died 1839; buried in Shurte cemetery, near LaGrange;
grave marked, Oct. 2, 1915, by Algonquin chapter,
St. Joseph and Benton Harbor, Mich.
Revolutionary service claimed.
Data recorded by Algonquin chapter, St. Joseph and
Benton Harbor, Mich.

STEPHEN MACK

MACK, Stephen. Born at Lyme, Conn., 1764.
Died Nov. 11, 1826; buried first, on east side of river,
south of Pike St.; second, Oak Hill cemetery, Pontiac;
grave marked, July 1, 1907, by General Richardson
chapter, Pontiac.

Son of Solomon Mack.

Stephen Mack married Temperence Bond of Gilsum.
Children:—There were twelve children, the following
  names are recorded: Stephen, b. 1798; John; Almon,
  b. 1805; Almira, b. 1805; Lovicy; Lavina, b. 1795;
  Harriet; Adsoah; Ruth; Rhoda.
Places of residence:—Gilsum, N. H.; Montague, N. H.;
  Tunbridge, Vt.; Norwich, Vt.; Detroit and Pontiac,
  Mich.
Revolutionary Service:—Enlisted at age of sixteen in
  New Hampshire militia, as a private in Capt. John
  Trotter's company under Col. Rufus Putnam's sixth
  regiment; received rank of colonel in Vermont troops.
Came to Michigan about 1810; located in Detroit.
  Family came to Mich., 1822.
Occupation:—Director of Bank of Mich., 1818; trustee
  of village of Detroit and supervisor 1816-'18.
Authorities quoted:—*History of Oakland County*, I, 75;
  Mass. Soldiers and Sailors in Revolution, X, 109;
  Mich. Hist. Colls., I, 24, 470; III, 223, 267, 570, 571,
  574; IV, 190, 459; V, 540; VI, 385; XIII, 316.   See
  also index volume to *Collections*.

CALEB BAKER MERRILL

MERRILL, Caleb Baker.   Born at Great Barrington,
  Mass., 1754.
Died July 2, 1842 at Springfield, Mich.; buried at
  Clarkston; grave marked, Sept. 17, 1908, by General
  Richardson chapter, Pontiac.
Married Sally Jackson, dau. of Col. Giles and Anna
  (Thomas) Jackson.   Sally (Jackson) Merrill was
  born Oct. 3, 1766; d. July 22, 186-.
Children:—John Jackson, b. 1797, d. 1866; Charlotte,
  b. 1804, d. 1873; Charles; Helen; Anna.

Revolutionary Service:—Was a commissioned officer in battles of Bennington, Bemis Heights, Saratoga, Stillwater, and at surrender of Burgoyne.
Came to Michigan, in 1833; located at Springfield, Oakland Co.
Data recorded by Mrs. Lillian Drake Avery.

SAMUEL NILES

NILES, Samuel. Born in the State of R. I.
Died July, 1838; buried Crook cemetery, Troy Twp.; grave marked, July 19, 1912, by General Richardson chapter.
Children:—The records mention a son by the name of Johnson.
Revolutionary Service:—Private under Gen. Green; was wounded in action.
Came to Mich., 1835; located with son Johnson Niles, the first white settler in twp. of Troy.
Data recorded by Mrs. Lillian Drake Avery, Pontiac.

EDWARD OTIS

OTIS, Edward. Born at Lynn, Conn., Apr. 6, 1766.
Died in Indiana, 1851; buried at Buchanan; grave marked, June 4, 1914, by Fort St. Joseph chapter, Niles.
Son of Robert and Mary (Stafford) Otis.
Married Mary Merrill, born 1770 in Vermont; died at Bigelows Mills, Ind.
Revolutionary Service:—Enlisted when fifteen years of age as private in Conn. troops; served eleven months, part of the time under Capt. Lord and Col. Staat.
Brought to Michigan for burial.

58   MICHIGAN MILITARY RECORDS

Profession:—Clergyman.
ata recorded by Fort St. Joseph chapter, Niles.

WILLIAM PANGBORN

PANGBORN, William.   Born 1742.
Died Mar. 10, 1852; aged 110; grave marked, May 22,
    1910, by Stevens Thomson Mason chapter, Ionia.
Revolutionary Service:—Enlisted at Newport, May 1,
    1779; fought under Washington through the Revolu-
    tion.   In Jan., 1781, transferred to Capt. Theodosus
    Towlus' company of 2nd New Jersey, commanded by
    Col. Philip Cortland; was a prisoner.   Served through
    the war of 1812.
Data recorded by Stevens Thomson Mason chapter,
    Ionia.
Ed. note:—See Pensioners of Territorial Michigan.

JOSEPH PARDY

PARDY, Joseph.
Buried in Oakridge cemetery, Marshall, Mich.; grave
    not marked.
Name recorded by the Mary Marshall chapter, Mar-
    shall, Mich.

EZRA PARKER

PARKER, Ezra.   Born at Wallingford, Conn., Dec. 13,
    1745.
Died July 7, 1842; buried in Royal Oak cemetery;
    grave marked, June 10, 1900, by General Richardson
    chapter, Pontiac.
Son of Andrew Parker.

Ezra Parker married 1st, Sarah Tuttle; 2nd,Elizabeth Perry.

Children:—Samuel; David; Ezra; Wm. M.; Joel; Cratus; Elizabeth; Ira; Abigail; infant son.

Places of residence:—Wallingford, Conn.; Adams, Mass., 1770; Herkimer Co., N. Y.; Bridgewater, N. Y.; Saugersfield Co., N. Y.; Royal Oak, Mich.

Revolutionary Service:—Grave stone inscribed "Revolutionary soldier". Was in battles of Bunker Hill and of Lexington, in Berkshire Co., Mass., militia; sergt. in Arnold's expedition through Maine and Quebec; in battles of Bennington and Saratoga.

Came to Michigan, June, 1835; located at Royal Oak, Oakland Co., Mich.

Data recorded by Mrs. Lillian Drake Avery, Pontiac.

Ed. note:—See also *Mich. Hist. Colls.*, VI, 255.

SELAH PECK

Peck, Selah.

Died 1859; buried at Athens; grave marked, May 13, 1916, by Battle Creek chapter, Battle Creek, Mich.

Married Temperance Wilcox, dau. of Benj. Wilcox of Bristol, Conn.

Children:—Eleazar, b. Jan. 6, 1793; Van Renslaer, b. 1800, lived in Camden, N. Y.; Harriet, m. Isham Simons of Athens, Mich.; Amey, m. David Hitchcock; Caroline, m. Joel Hitchcock; Sophia, m. Smith White.

Selah Peck was the son of Eleazar and Elizabeth (Woodbury) Peck.

Places of residence:—Southington, Hartford Co., Conn.; Greenbush, N. Y.; Camden, N. Y.

Revolutionary Service:—A drummer in theRevolution.

Data recorded by Battle Creek chapter, and also Mrs. Lillian D. Avery, Pontiac.

JOHN PETTIGREW

PETTIGREW, (Petticrew), John. Born 1757, Virginia. Died 1838; buried in Union cemetery, La Grange Twp., near Niles, Cass Co., Mich.; grave marked, June 25, 1915, by Algonquin chapter, St. Joseph and Benton Harbor.

Children:—There were nine children.

Living descendants recorded, 1918:—Mrs. Wm. Smith, Benton Harbor, Mich; Mrs. Henry Kinnerle, Cassopolis; Mrs. E. King, Cassopolis.

Revolutionary Service:—Served the entire period of Revolutionary war; and was also a soldier of the war of 1812.

Came to Michigan, 1829; located near Cassopolis, Cass Co.

Data recorded by Algonquin chapter, St. Joseph and Benton Harbor.

JACOB PETTY

PETTY, Jacob.

Died 1838; buried Sashabaw Plains, Oakland Co.; grave located, Oct. 2, 1915, General Richardson chapter, Pontiac.

Revolutionary Service:—Claimed to have belonged to Washington's Body Guard.

Places of residence:—An early resident of Independence Twp., Oakland Co., Mich.

Data recorded by Mrs. Lillian Drake Avery, Pontiac.

JOEL PHELPS

PHELPS, Joel. Born July 16, 1755.

Buried, Rose Corners, Oakland Co., Mich.; grave located by General Richardson chapter, Pontiac.

Married Anner, born 1767.

Children:—Gilbert, b. Dec., 1788; Minerva, b. Dec., 1790; Othanile, b. 1793; Martha, b. 1795; Sarah, b. 1798; Joel, b. 1800; Daniel, b. 1802; Mariah, b. 1804; Aaron, b. 1806; Lewis, b. 1809; Henry, b. 1813; Stephen, b. 1815.

Places of residence:—Bloomfield, N. Y.; Oakland Co., Mich.

Revolutionary Service:--Enlisted June, 1775 in Mass., Capt. John McKinstry's company, Col. John Patterson's Mass. reg.; served in Capt. Hall's company, under Col. Henry Sherbourn, 1777; Capt. Stephen Hardin's company, under Col. Zebulon Butler, Conn. reg.; Quartermaster in Gen. Burgoyne's army of Va.; later in commissary dept.; in battles of Cedars, Trenton, Princeton, Bound Brook, Wyoming; was a pensioner.

Came to Michigan, 1836; located Oakland Co., Mich.

Data recorded by Mrs. Lillian D. Avery.

MOSES PORTER

Porter, Moses.

Buried in Metamora cemetery, Lapeer Co., Mich.; grave marked, Oct. 28, 1907, by General Richardson chapter, Pontiac.

Data recorded by Mrs. Lillian Drake Avery, Pontiac.

BENIAH POST

Post, Beniah.

"Soldier of the Revolution."

Name officially recorded by Sarah Caswell Angell chapter, Ann Arbor, Mich.

LYDIA POTTER

POTTER, Lydia (Barnes).
Died Aug., 1836; buried in Baldwin cemetery, Avon
    Twp.; grave marked, Aug. 19, 1911, by General
    Richardson chapter, Pontiac.
Married Lemuel Potter who died Feb. 26, 1836; buried
    in Chili, N. Y.
Descendants: — Marilla Hemingway; granddaughter,
    Mrs. Abigail H. McArthur.
Revolutionary Service:—"She worked night and day
    for the destitute soldiers at Valley Forge."
Came to Michigan about 1826; located at Paint Creek,
    Oakland Co., Mich.; lived with dau., Mrs. Marilla
    Hemingway.
Data recorded by Mrs. Lillian D. Avery, Pontiac.
Remarks:—"Lemuel Potter was a soldier of the Revo-
    lution and as a corporal engaged in securing pro-
    visions for Washington's destitute soldiers—met
    Lydia Barnes who later became his wife."

CALEB PRATT

PRATT, Caleb. Born 1760.
Buried in Oakland Co.
Revolutionary Service:—"Under Stark at Bennington."
Came to Mich., with son, Capt. John W. Pratt, of
    Springfield.
Name recorded by Mrs. Lillian D. Avery, Pontiac.
Remarks:—"In the course of a long and active life
    was frequently called by his fellow citizens to fill
    offices both civil and military and he discharged the
    duties thereof with honor to himself and satisfac-
    tion to the public." Pontiac *Jacksonian*, June 13,
    1843

STEPHEN PRATT

PRATT, Stephen. Born in the State of Mass., Dec. 17, 1764.

Died Aug. 3, 1854; buried, Mountain Home, Otsego, Mich.; grave marked, May 23, 1917, by Hannah McIntosh Cady chapter, Allegan.

Married to Rhoda Sherwood, b. Aug. 29, 1770, Mass.

Children:—Milton; Stephen; John; Jerrod; Katie.

Places of residence:—Mass.; Pownal, Vt.; Sardinia, N. Y.; Barry Co., Mich.

Revolutionary Service:—Enlisted, May or June, 1781, at Pownal, Vt., under Capt. Wm. Huchins, and Major Ebenezar Allen; 1782, under Capt. Wm. Huchins, Col. Bronson, and Major Ebenezar Allen.

Came to Michigan, 1849; located in Barry Co.

Baptist minister and missionary to Indians.

Data recorded by Hannah McIntosh Cady chapter, Allegan.

Ed. note:—*Mich. Hist. Colls.*, XXXI, 105, gives name of a son, Horace.

JOHN QUICK

QUICK, John. Born in N. J., 1760.

Died 1851; buried in Laphan cemetery, Maple Grove; grave marked by Emily Virginia Mason chapter, Hastings, Mich.

Children:—Abraham S.

Places of residence:—Penn., Canada, and N. Y., before coming to Michigan.

Revolutionary Service:—John Quick served under Washington in N. J. and was in Pa. campaigns.

Came to Michigan, 1842; located in Maple Grove Twp., Barry Co.; lived on farm with his son Abraham S.

Data recorded by Emily Virginia Mason chapter, Hastings, Mich.

EZEKIEL RANSOM

RANSOM, Major Ezekiel. Born at Colchester, Conn., Oct. 1, 1763.

Died Nov. 1, 1838; buried at Mountain Home, Kalamazoo, Mich.; grave marked, May 30, 1907, by Lucinda Hinsdale Stone chapter, Kalamazoo, Mich.

Son of Newton and Sarah (Jones) Ransom.

Married Lucinda Fletcher, dau. of Gen. Samuel and Mehitable Fletcher, Mar. 25, 1791, at Townshend, Vt.

Children:—Miranda, b. Sept. 6, 1792, Newfane, Vt., d. Jan., 1872, Mooers, N. Y., m. Elijah Ransom; Philanda, b. Feb. 23, 1794, Townshend, Vt., d. Sept., 1847, Middleburg, Vt., m. Jonathan Allen; Fanny Jones, b. Jan. 7, 1796, Shelburne Falls, Mass., d. Jan. 16, 1878, Chicago, Ill., m. John P. Marsh, Dec. 7, 1817; Epaphroditus, b. Mar. 24, 1798, Shelburne Falls, Mass., d. Nov. 12, 1859, Fort Scott, Kansas, m. Almira C. Ransom, Feb. 21, 1827; Fletcher, b. Aug. 22, 1800, Townshend, Vt., d. June 3, 1867, m. Elizabeth Noves, June 28, 1831; Roswell, b. Nov. 21, 1802, Townshend, Vt., d. Nov. 17, 1877, Galesburg, Mich., m. Wealthy I. Shafter, 1830; Alexis, b. July 21, 1805, Townshend, Vt., d. Jan. 15, 1888, Kalamazoo, Mich., m. (1st), Lois H. Stone, Nov. 15, 1835, (2nd), Mrs. Nancy Brown, Warren, Ohio; Sophia, b. Feb. 15, 1807, Townshend, Vt., d. Aug. 19, 1887, Kalamazoo, Mich., m. Amariah I. Prouty, Nov. 28, 1828; Clarissa, b. Dec. 30, 1808, Townshend, Vt., d. June 23, 1840, Kalamazoo, Mich., m. Rev.

Jeremiah Hall, D.D., Sept. 28, 1830; Samuel, b. Dec. 23, 1810, Townshend, Vt., d. June 21, 1876, Waukesha, Wis., m. Eleanor B. Goddard, July, 1839; Lucinda, b. Dec. 7, 1812, Townshend, Vt., d. Dec. 28, 1899, Highland Park, Ill., m. Allen Goodridge, Nov. 9, 1833; James W., b. Aug. 8, 1816, Townshend, Vt., d. 1839, Kalamazoo, Mich.

Places of residence:—Colchester, Conn.; Shelburne Falls, Mass.

Revolutionary Service:—Enlisted, 1777, with Vt. militia; fought at Crown Point and in battles of Bennington and Saratoga; present at Burgoyne's surrender; non-com. officer on the staff of Gen. George Washington.

Major Ezekiel Ransom distinguished himself in the war of 1812.

Occupation:—Farmer and general trader.

Remarks:—1st deacon of Baptist church, Kalamazoo, and was instrumental in founding Huron Literary Institute, afterward Kalamazoo College.

Came to Michigan., 1835; owned a farm, the dwelling now on Park and Academy St.

Data recorded by Lucinda Hinsdale Stone chapter, Kalamazoo, Mich.

Authorities quoted:—*History of First Baptist Church of Kalamazoo*, by Rev. John E. Smith; *Ransom Genealogy*.

Ed. note:—*Mich. Hist. Colls.*, XIV, 115, gives "Wells" as name of youngest son.

ELEAZOR ROOT

Root, Eleazor. Born 1764.
Buried in Oak Grove cemetery, Manchester; grave

marked, May, 1908, by Sarah Caswell Angell chapter, Ann Arbor, Mich.

Descendants:—Grandson, Ed. E. Root, Manchester, Mich.

Revolutionary Service:—Enlisted, 1779, at age of 15; served one year.

Data recorded by Sarah Caswell Angell chap ɛr, Ann Arbor, Mich.

JONATHAN SAMPSON.

SAMPSON, Jonathan, jr.

Son of Jonathan and Deborah (Bradford) Sampson. Jonathan, Sr., b. Apr. 3, 1727; lost at sea. Deborah Bradford, b. Nov. 18 1732; d. 1820; great-granddaughter of Gov. Wm. Bradford.

Children of Jonathan, Jr.:—Lucy Sampson, m. Pratt and was the grandmother of Mrs. Emma Hunn, Mrs. Clara Bogie, and Mrs. Cora M. Shaw.

Revolutionary Service:-Minute man in the Revolution. Jonathan Sampson, Jr., was brother of Deborah (Sampson) Gannett, who served as Robert Shurtliff in the Revolution.

Lived near Hillsdale, Mich.; tradition claims his burial in Michigan; place not located.

Data recorded by Mrs. L. E. Holland, Saginaw, Mich.

Ed. note:—Relatives living in Saginaw: Mrs. Emma Hunn; Mrs. Olive Boyd, dau. of Mrs. Cora M. Shaw; and Miss Bell Chandler, a dau. of Mrs. Boyd. Other relatives living in Mich. are: Mrs. Clara A. Bogie, her two daughters, Bell and Lena; Horace, and Elizabeth Sampson who live near Allegan, Mich. Deborah, a sister of Jonathan, was the patriot who served as "Robert Shurtleff" a private in the Revo-

lution, for the period of three years. "So trust-
worthy, and fearless, that she was appointed aide-
de-camp to Gen. Patterson." Deborah married
Capt. Benjamin Gannett, of Sharon, 1784. Gen.
Washington is said to have attended the wedding.
Mrs. Gannett died April 29, 1827. A full account of
her life may be found in the *National D. A. R.
Magazine*, Sept.–Oct., 1917.

JEREMIAH SELKIRK (SELKRIG OR "SILKRAGS")

SELKIRK, Jeremiah. Born in England (also recorded
as N. Y.).
Buried, Wayland Twp., farm on bank of Selkirk lake,
Allegan Co.; grave marked, Sept. 1, 1911 (recorded
also as Aug., 1911), by Hannah McIntosh Cady
chapter, Allegan, Mich.
Name of son, James.[7]
Places of residence:—Rochester, N. Y.; Wayland Twp.,
Allegan Co., Mich.
Revolutionary Service:—Aide-de-camp to Washing-
ton; "Fought under the name of Silkrags, under
which name he was pensioned." "After the death
of his wife, at Rochester, N. Y., Jeremiah S. immi-
grated to Michigan, and lived with his son James, an
ordained Episcopal minister, sent to Allegan Co.,
from the mission at Niles."
Data recorded by Mrs. Winona Moore Sherwood and
Mrs. Anna W. Tripp, Allegan, Mich.
Ed. note:—The James Selkirk record follows:
Children:—James E., d. 1901; Jeremiah, killed at Crow
Wing, Minn., 1858; Charles, d. Nov. 19, 1860, at age

---

7. Rev. James Selkirk was born at Claverack, N. Y., Nov. 15, 1790.
Died Oct. 5, 1877; buried beside Jeremiah Selkirk, on Wayland
Co. farm; grave marked, Sept. 1, 1911, by Hannah McIntosh
Cady chapter, Allegan, Mich.

of twenty-two. James Selkirk immigrated to Michigan, 1839; located at Griswold mission, Wayland Twp., Allegan Co., on sections 20 and 27; was an Episcopal missionary to the Ottawas and Pottawottomi, under Chief Saginaw, in the vicinity of Gun Lake. *Mich. Hist. Colls.*, V, 381. Rev. James Selkrig was peacemaker between the Ottawas on Grand River and Pottawottomi on Kalamazoo. He translated book of Common Prayer into Indian language, a copy of which is now in the possession of Mrs. W M. Sherwood, Allegan. Rev. Selkrig was also noted as a musician. He built an organ which is now the property of Hannah McIntosh Cady chapter, Allegan, Mich. Served in the war of 1812. Rev. James Selkirk was a 33rd degree Mason. *Mich. Hist. Colls.*, XXXII, 383.

JAMES SELLICK

SELLICK, James. · Born in the State of Conn., in 1763. Died 1851; buried in Allen cemetery, Silver Creek Twp., Cass Co.; grave marked, June 25, 1915, by Algonquin chapter of St. Joseph and Benton Harbor, Mich.

Children:—Mary; Hezekiah (born in Conn.).

Name of living relative (1918), James Sellick Richards, Dowagiac, R. F. D.

Came to Michigan, and located in Silver Creek Twp.

Data recorded by Mrs. Grace V. Canaran of Algonquin chapter, St. Joseph and Benton Harbor, Mich.

BENJAMIN SMITH

See Benjamin Bulson.

FRANCIS SMITH

SMITH, Francis, physician.

Buried in Benton cemetery, near Saline, Mich.; grave marked, July 10, 1913, by Ypsilanti chapter, Ypsilanti, Mich.

Data recorded by Ypsilanti chapter.

ITHAMAR SMITH

SMITH, Ithamar. Born in Long Meadow, Mass., Jan. 13, 1756.

Died Sept. 1, 1844; buried in Oak Hill cemetery, Pontiac, Mich; grave marked, July 1, 1907, by General Richardson chapter, Pontiac, Mich.

Married Lucy Nevers, Jan. 26, 1780; died Sept. 25, 1843.

Ithamar Smith's father's name was John.

Children:—Roderick, b. Mar. 10, 1781; Henry, b. Apr. 19, 1782; Henry, b. Feb. 17, 1784; Sally, b. Mar. 5, 1786; Sarah, b. Jan. 23, 1787, d. Feb. 8, 1876, Pontiac, Mich.; Fanny, b. Jan. 12, 1789, d. Mar., 1858, Pontiac, Mich.; John Morgan, b. Dec. 31, 1790, d. Oct. 26, 1864, Grand Rapids, Mich.; Eleazer, b. Oct. 21, 1792, d. Nov. 23, 1797; Hannah Morgan, b. June 17, 1794, d. May 1, 1851, Pontiac, Mich.; Louis Nevis, b. Mar. 21, 1796, d. May, 1796; Dr. Geo., b. Aug. 19, 1797, d. Aug. 25, 1844, Syracuse; Lucy, b. Apr. 17, 1799, d. July 8, 1837, Pontiac, Mich.; Eleazer, b. Nov. 25, 1801, d. May 22, 1802.

Places of residence:—Wilbramham, Hampshire Co., Mass.

Revolutionary Service:—Enlisted, June, 1776, for 6 months, private in Capt. Josiah Smith's company,

Col. Whitney's reg.; in Apr., 1777, as an artificer in
Capt. Richard Faxon's company, Col. David Mason's
reg.; 1779, quartermaster shop at Springfield, Mass.,
under Col. Wm. Smith.

Authorities quoted:—*History of Oakland County.*, Vol.
I, ch. 6.

Data recorded by Mrs. Lillian D. Avery, Pontiac,
Mich.

REUBEN SMITH

SMITH, Reuben.

Buried near Marine City; grave marked, Aug. 23, 1915,
by Ot-si-ke-ta chapter, St. Clair.

Data recorded by Ot-si-ke-ta chapter, St. Clair, Mich.

Ed. note:—See Pensioners of Territorial Michigan.

GEORGE SORTER

SORTER, George.   Born 1756.

Died Sept. 14, 1851 "aged ninety-five"; buried at
Raisinville cemetery six miles south of Monroe, south
side of Raisin River; grave reported by the Sarah
Caswell Angell chapter, Ann Arbor, Mich.

Children:—John, b. 1818, d. 1895.

Place of residence:—Ovid, Seneca Co., N. Y.

Revolutionary Service:—"Drove provision wagon four
years; carried gun, two years."

Data recorded by Mrs. William Henry Wait, Ann
Arbor, Mich.

Mich. Hist. Colls., XXVII, 163, gives the following
statement:—"His (John Sorter's) father was George
Sorter, a soldier in the Revolutionary army." "He
sprang from an old Pennsylvania Dutch family who

trace their origin back many generations and include in them a number of New York's noted men and honored women."

SILAS SPRAGUE

SPRAGUE, Silas.   Born in Conn., Feb. 18, 1762.

Died in Troy, Mich., Mar. 8, 1841; buried in Crooks cemetery, Troy Twp., Oakland Co., Mich.; grave marked, July 19, 1912, by General Richardson chapter, Pontiac, Mich.

Married Polly Leonard, who was born Oct. 16, 1763, d. Oct. 5, 1813, in the State of New York.

Children:—Silas, b. 1785; Polly, b. 1790; Charles, b. 1791; Thomas, b. 1794; Orrin, b. 179–; Barnabas, b. 1799; John, b. 1801; Leonard, b. 1804.

Revolutionary Service:—Mustered, July, 1779, from Great Barrington, Capt. Goodrich's company, Col. Ashley's reg.; also served for the town of Stillwater, 1781; a major in the Toledo War.

Came to Michigan in 1824; located in Oakland Co.; lived with son Silas Sprague.

Authorities quoted:—*Mass. Soldiers and Sailors*; *History of Oakland Co.*, ch. 6, p. 88; *Mich. Hist. Colls.*, XIV, 585; III, 569.

Ed. note:—See also Pensioners of Territorial Michigan.

JAMES STEVENS

STEVENS, James.   Born 1756.

Died July 8, 1846; buried in Arlington cemetery, (near) Lawrence, Van Buren Co., Mich.; grave marked, June 11, 1915, by Algonquin chapter of St. Joseph and Benton Harbor, Mich.

Places of residence:—Came to Michigan from New
York; located in Van Buren Co.
Revolutionary Service:—Under Washington.
Authorities quoted:—*News Palladium*, June 11, 1915.
Data recorded by Mrs. Grace V. Canaran, St. Joseph,
Mich.

WILBUR SWEET

SWEET, Wilbur. Born in State of Vermont, 1760.
Died at Kalamazoo, Mich., Aug. 19, 1857; place of
burial under investigation.
Revolutionary Service:—"Served as a boy in the army
of the Revolution and as a man throughout the entire
war of 1812."
Came to Michigan, 1818; located at Kalamazoo.
Authorities quoted:—*Red Book of Michigan*, 1871.
Data recorded by Sue I. Silliman, Three Rivers.

JOHN TERHUNE

TERHUNE, John. Born at Hackensack, N. J.
Buried in Emily Whitmore Park cemetery, Washtenaw
Co., Mich.; grave marked by Sarah Caswell Angell
chapter, of Ann Arbor, and the Ypsilanti chapter,
Ypsilanti, Mich.
Married Sarah Vreeland.
Revolutionary Service:—Sergeant and ensign in Revo-
lutionary war; served in Capt. John Intwater's
company, N. Y.
Came to Michigan, 1831; located at Carpenters Cor-
ners, Pittsfield.
Data recorded by Mrs. William H. Wait, Ann Arbor,
Mich.

SARAH (VREELAND) TERHUNE

TERHUNE, Sarah (Vreeland).

Buried in Emily Whitmore Park cemetery, Washtenaw Co.; grave marked by Sarah Caswell Angell chapter, Ann Arbor, and the Ypsilanti chapter, Ypsilanti, Mich.

Married John Terhune.

Revolutionary Service:—"Sarah Terhune walked nine miles before dawn to warn the American camp of the approach of the British who had encamped the night before on a corner of her father's plantation at Hackensack." The young soldier to whom she delivered the message afterwards became her husband.

Data recorded by Mrs. William H. Wait, Ann Arbor, Mich.

WILLIAM NATHAN TERRY

TERRY, William Nathan. Born 1760.

Died Jan. 20, 1840; buried, Charles Terry lot, Oak Hill cemetery, Pontiac; grave marked, Oct. 1, 1909, by General Richardson chapter, Pontiac, Mich.

Married Eleanor Lewis, who was born about 1776 and died Aug. 25, 1849.

Children:—Charles, b. 1802, d. July 3, 1854; Sarah Lee, b. Oct. 27, 1806, d. June 13, 1899; Ellen; William; Jacob; Joshua; John; Merritt; Caleb; Polly; Barney.

Revolutionary Service:—Enlisted Mar., 1774; was in the battle of Bunker Hill, 1775, in Capt. Ransom's company, Pa. troops, under Col. Butler; served until Oct., 1782.

Came to Michigan, 1824; located on Saginaw turnpike, two miles north of Pontiac, Mich.

Data recorded by Mrs. Lillian D. Avery, Pontiac.
"William Nathan Terry made his declaration, Nov. 10,
1828, at the age of sixty-eight."
Ed. note:—See also Pensioners of Territorial Michigan.

ZOETH TOBY

Toby, Zoeth. Born in Dartmouth, Mass., Dec. 30,
1758.
Died 1838; buried in the Lawler cemetery, Charleston
Twp., Kalamazoo Co.; grave marked by Lucinda
Hindsdale Stone chapter, May 30, 1917.
Revolutionary Service:—"Private Toby enlisted 1780;
was wounded and honorably discharged, 1781."
Data recorded by Mrs. William A. Stone, Kalamazoo,
Mich.
Ed. note:—The N. S. D. A. R. membership papers,
belonging to Miss Hazel Hughes of the Abiel Fellows
chapter, Three Rivers, record the following data concerning Zoeth Toby from whom Miss Hughes is a
direct descendant: Zoeth Toby enlisted from Dartmouth, Mass.; served until 1781. He married
Abegail Keene. Children: Betsey; Silvey, m. Newton; Katie, m. Dennison; Zackeus; Hannah; Polly,
m. Levi Blakesh; Louise, m. Emeline Jackobs; Benjamin, b. Nov. 19, 1796, m. Louisa Wood; Sophy, b.
June 22, 1803, m. Lucius Lindsey; Caroline, b. Dec.
22, 1804, m. Lunkford Burdick. Died at Plainwell,
Mich., Aug. 21, 1838.
Authorities quoted:—Rickton's *History of New Bedford, Mass.*, p. 383; N. S. D. A. R. numbers 91796,
101316, 110612, 120316.

JOSEPH TODD

Todd, Joseph. Born in Warsaw, N. Y., Feb. 11, 1765.
Buried in Oak Hill cemetery, Pontiac; grave marked,
July 1, 1907, by General Richardson chapter,
Pontiac, Mich.
Son of 2nd Lt. Joseph Todd.
Married.
Children:—Elizabeth, b. 1791, d. 1846; Catherine, b.
1796, d. 1845; Julia; John; Joseph; Jonathan;
Samuel, b. 1804.
Places of residence:—Warsaw, N. Y.; Detroit, Mich.;
and Mt. Clemens, Mich.
Revolutionary Service:—Enlisted Apr., 1781. Private
in Capt. Peter Bertholft's company, Col. Henry
Wasner's reg., N. Y. militia.
Came to Michigan, 1818; located in Oakland Co..
Mich.
Data recorded by Mrs. Lillian D. Avery, Pontiac, Mich.
Ed. note:—See also Pensioners of Territorial Michigan.

JOHN TRUMBULL

Trumbull, John. Born at Waterbury, Conn., Apr.
13, 1750.
Died at Spring Wells, May 12, 1831; buried at Elm-
wood, Detroit; grave marked, June 14, 1916, by
Louisa St. Clair chapter, Detroit, Mich.
Son of John and Sarah (Whitman) Trumbull; Sarah
Whitman was the dau. of Rev. Samuel Whitman,
Farmington.
John Trumbull, Jr., married Sarah Hubbard, dau. of
Col. T. Everett and Sarah (Whitehead) Hubbard,
New Haven, Conn. Sarah (Hubbard) Trumbull,

was born May 31, 1758; died at Detroit, Sept. 5, 1835.

Children:—Samuel, b. Hartford, Conn., d. Detroit, Mich.; Juliana, b. Hartford, Conn., Apr. 23, 1786, d. Detroit, Mich., Feb. 19, 1860.

Profession:—Poet, lawyer, judge.

Places of residence:—Hartford, Conn.; Detroit, Mich.

Revolutionary Service:—Ranked as a Revolutionary patriot for his poem, "Mac Fingal" the "Hudubras" of the Revolution. "It was one of the forces of the Revolution because as a satire on the Tories, it penetrated into every farm house and sent the rustic volunteers laughing into the ranks of Washington." Came to Michigan, 1825; spent the declining years of his life with his dau., Juliana, the wife of Gov. William Woodbridge, Detroit, Mich.

Authorities:—Ezra Hyde genealogy, p. 923; *Mich. Hist. Colls.*

Data compiled by Mrs. Charles M. Metcalf, 728 Hickerson Ave., Detroit; recorded by Miss G. B. Krum, historian, Louisa St. Clair chapter, Detroit, Mich.

Ed. note:—"At the age of seven, John Trumbull was considered qualified to enter Yale college and in 1773 was admitted to the bar; was poet, lawyer, judge,—one of the most interesting characters of early Michigan." For character sketches of John Trumbull see Harper's *Monthly Magazine*, LII, 407; *Mich. Hist. Colls.*, II, 54.

JOSEPH VAN NETTER

VAN NETTER, Joseph. Born 1763.
Buried in Oakland Co.

Revolutionary Service:—Served in Capt. Wendell's company, Col. Wynkoop's reg., N. Y. troops; later under Col. Van Schaick; was in battles of Monmouth and Yorktown. First Revolutionary soldier to file an application for pension in Oakland Co. court. Was pensioned Feb. 22, 1822.

Came to Michigan 1840; located at Holly.

Data recorded by Mrs. Lillian D. Avery, Pontiac, Mich.

MARK WATKINS

WATKINS, Mark. Born Dec. 6, 1763,

Died June 21, 1836; buried at Leonidas, Mich.; grave marked, Sept. 23, 1916, by Abiel Fellows chapter, Three Rivers, Mich.

Married:—Esther Legg, July 15, 1784, at Patridgefield, Mass. She was born Jan. 11, 1764 and died Oct. 24, 1847.

Children:—Elijah; Orrin; Levi.

Mark Watkins was the son of Capt. Nathan and Sarah (Whitney) Watkins of Patridgefield, Mass.

Revolutionary Service:—Enlisted Jan. 1, 1776; 1777 at Patridgefield, Mass., in company with his father, in Col. Phinney's reg.; and also in Col. Samuel Brewer's reg., in 1780 under Col. Fellows and served until the close of the Revolution.

Came to Michigan, 1835; located at Leonidas, St. Joseph Co., Mich.

Occupation:—Farmer, millwright, carpenter.

Data compiled by Mrs. E. W. Watkins, Sherwood, Mich., and recorded by Dr. Blanche M. Haines, Three Rivers.

Remarks:—Levi, son of Mark, was married, July 4, 1805, to Silence Clarke and Apr. 29, 1809, to Lucinda

Duton.   He served in the war of 1812.   Edward
Wirt Watkins, a grandson of Levi, served two years
in the Civil War.

ZADOCK WELLMAN

WELLMAN, Zadoc.   Born 1761.
Buried "East of Troy Corners, Oakland Co., Mich.,"
Revolutionary Service:—Name on pension roll of 1840;
   age given as 79 and residence Troy at the home of
   Joel Wellman, Troy, Mich.
Name recorded by Mrs. Lillian Drake Avery, Pontiac,
   Mich.

JAMES WITHERELL

WITHERELL, James.   Born at Mansfield, Mass., June
   16, 1759.
Died at Detroit, Mich., Jan. 9, 1838; buried at Elm-
   wood, Detroit; grave marked, June 14, 1916, by
   Louisa St. Clair chapter, Detroit, Mich.
Son of Simon and Sarah (Gilbert) Witherell.
Married Amy Hawkins, dau. of Charles and Sarah
   (Olney) Hawkins; Amy (Hawkins) Witherell was
   born June 17, —— at Smithfield, R. I. and died
   Aug. 7, 1848, at Detroit.
Children:—James, b. 1791; Sarah; Myra, b. 1797;
   Betsey Matilda, b. 1793; Mary Amy, b. 1795; Benj.
   F. H., b. 1797; James B., b. 1799.
Revolutionary Service:—Enlisted, June, 1775, in Mass.
   reg., at age of sixteen, and served throughout the
   war of Revolution.   "Rose from private to rank of
   adj. in the 11th Mass.   Was in battles of White
   Plains, Long Island, Bemis Heights, at Valley Forge,
   Monmouth and surrender of Burgoyne."

Commandant of Detroit in absence of Hull in war of 1812.

Came to Michigan, 1808; located at Detroit. His family came to Michigan in 1810.

Profession:—Physician.

Government Service:—Associate judge; chief justice; member of Legislature from Rutland Co., Vt.; appointed by Jefferson in 1807 as judge of supreme court of Territory of Michigan; in 1827–1830 was secretary of Territory.

Data compiled by Miss Mary R. Lacey, 628 Jefferson Ave., Detroit.

Ed. note:—See also Pensioners of Territorial Michigan.

NATHAN WOOD

Wood, Nathan. Born 1760.

Died Dec. 10, 1846; buried at Riverside cemetery, Albion; grave marked, Oct. 17, 1908, by Hannah Tracy Grant chapter, Albion.

Son of Benjamin Wood.

Nathan Wood married Lucy Hammond.

Children:—Lydia; Benjamin; Nathan, Jr.; Polly; Martin B.

Resided in Chenango Valley, N. Y.

Revolutionary Service:—"At the age of twelve years was a body servant to his father, Benjamin Wood, and served through the Revolution."

Data recorded by Mrs. W. H. Rogers, Albion, Mich.

BENJAMIN WOODRUFF

Woodruff, Benjamin. Born at Morristown, N. J., Nov. 26, 1744.

Died Oct. 18, 1837; buried Forest Hill cemetery, Ann
   Arbor; grave marked, May, 1906, by Sarah Caswell
   Angell chapter, Ann Arbor, Mich.
Revolutionary Service:—Served as a drummer for
   eighteen months under Capt. Ward Thomas.
Ed. note:—Year of death is also recorded as 1835.
   Woodruff's Grove, one mile from Ypsilanti, was
   named for Benjamin Woodruff. *Mich. Hist. Colls.*,
   XXXVI, 519.
Data recorded by Sarah Caswell Angell chapter, Ann
   Arbor, Mich.

GENERAL ALEXANDER MACOMB,
Commander-in-Chief of the American Army at Plattsburg.

PENSIONERS OF TERRITORIAL MICHIGAN

There is a distinctive pathos about the lives of the Revolutionary soldiers whom Michigan may claim, for, in almost every instance, it is an old man, breaking the ties of a life time, who follows the trail of sturdy children or grandchildren to a home in the wilderness; and the indirect testimony gleaned from the laws, under which the soldiers were pensioned, deepens the growing conviction that not the least courageous act, in the life of a soldier of 1776, was his immigration to territorial Michigan.

CHAPTER II

PENSIONERS OF TERRITORIAL MICHIGAN

ESTABLISHMENT OF THE PENSION LAWS, AND THE RESOLUTION BY THE SENATE, IN 1835, THAT THE NAMES OF PENSIONERS BY STATE AND COUNTY BE PUBLISHED.

The first pension law, in behalf of the soldiers and sailors fighting for the principles of liberty, in the days of the Revolution was passed by the Continental Congress, Aug. 26, 1776.

"WHEREAS, in course of the present war, some commissioned and non-commissioned officers of the army and navy, as also private soldiers, marines and seamen, may lose a limb, or be otherwise so disabled as to prevent them serving in the army or navy, or getting their livelihood, and may stand in need of relief:

"*Resolved*, that every commissioned officer, non-commissioned officer, and private soldier, who shall lose a limb in any engagement, or be so disabled in the service of the United States of America as to render him incapable afterwards of getting a livelihood, shall receive during his life, or the continuance of such disability, the one-half of his monthly pay from and after the time that his pay as an officer or soldier ceases; to be paid by the Committee as hereafter mentioned.

"That every commander of every ship of war or armed vessel, commissioned officer, warrant officer, marine or seaman, belonging to the United States of America, who shall lose a limb in any engagement, in

which no prize shall be taken, or be therein otherwise
so disabled as to be rendered incapable of getting a
livelihood, shall receive during his life, or the continuance of such disability, the one-half of his monthly
pay, from and after the time that his pay as an officer
or marine or seaman ceases; to be paid as hereafter
mentioned. But, in case a prize shall be taken at
the time such loss of limb or other disability shall
happen, then such sum as he may receive out of the
net profits of such prize, before a dividend is made of
the same, agreeable to former orders of Congress, shall
be considered as part of his half pay, and computed
accordingly.

"That every commissioned officer, non-commissioned
officer, and private soldier, in the army, and every
commander, commissioned officer, warrant officer,
marine, or seaman of any of the ships of war, or armed
vessels belonging to the United States of America, who
shall be wounded in any engagement, so as to be rendered incapable of serving in the army or navy, though
not totally disabled from getting a livelihood, shall
receive such monthly sum towards his subsistence as
shall be judged adequate by the assembly or other
representative body of the State where he belongs or
resides, upon application to them for that purpose,
provided the same does not exceed his half pay.

"Provided, that no commissioned officer, non-commissioned officer, and private soldier, in the army, commander, commissioned officer, warrant officer, marine
or seaman of any of the ships of war, or armed vessels
belonging to the United States of America, who shall
be wounded or disabled as aforesaid, shall be entitled
to his half pay or other allowance, unless he produce to
the committee or officer appointed to receive the same,

in the state where he resides or belongs or to the assembly or legislative body of such State, a certificate from the commanding officer, who was in the same engagement in which he was so wounded, or, in case of his death, from some other officer of the same corps, and the surgeon that attended him, or a certificate from the commander of the ship of war or armed vessel engaged in the action, in which any officer, marine, or seaman, received his wound, and from the surgeon who attended him, of the name of the person so wounded, his office, rank, department, regiment, company, ship of war, or armed vessel, to which he belonged, his office or rank therein, the nature of his wound, and in what action or engagement he received it.

"That it be recommended to the several assemblies or legislative bodies of the United States of America, to appoint some person or persons in their respective states who shall receive and examine all such certificates, as may be presented to them and register the same in a book, and also what support is adjudged by the assembly or legislative body of their state, to those whose case requires but a partial support, and also of the payment from time to time of every half-pay and other allowance, and of the death of such disabled person, or ceasing of such allowance, and shall make a fair and regular report of the same quarterly to the Secretary of Congress or Board of War, where a separate record shall be kept of the same.

"That it be recommended to the assemblies or legislative bodies of the several states, to cause payment to be made of all such half-pay or other allowances as shall be adjudged due to the persons aforenamed on account of the United States.

"Provided, that all such officers and soldiers that may be entitled to the aforesaid pension, and are found to be capable of doing guard or garrison duty, shall be formed in a corps of invalids, and subject to the said duty; and all officers, marines, and seaman of the navy who shall be entitled to the pension aforesaid, and shall be found capable of doing any duty on board the navy, or any department thereof, shall be liable to be so employed. Ordered that the above be published."

September 25, 1778, the following resolutions were approved, "That, whereas, divers of officers, and others, have lost limbs, or been otherwise disabled as aforesaid, before the 26th of August, to whom the like relief ought equitably to be extended," it was therefore resolved that the above mentioned pension or privilege of half pay should be extended to all who should have lost limbs "or been otherwise disabled in the service of the United Colonies or States, before the said 26th of August, and since the commencement of hostilities on the 19th of April 1775.

"And, Whereas, doubts may arise in some cases whether certain persons maimed or disabled and claiming pensions, were at the time in the service of the said Colonies or States, for removing the same,

"*Resolved*, that every commissioned and non-commissioned officer and private man, who since the commencement of hostilities, as aforesaid, has been, or hereafter shall be, drawn for the common defense (and not for the service of any particular State), or who has turned out, or shall hereafter turn out, voluntarily, to oppose the enemies of the United Colonies or States, upon any sudden attack or invasion, or upon any enterprise carried on under their authority, and in such service has lost or shall lose a limb, or has been, or shall be otherwise disabled as aforesaid, shall be entitled to the pension allowed in the said resolve of the 26th of August, 1776; provided that any such commissioned officer or non-commissioned officer or private man, being found capable of doing guard or garrison duty, shall be subject thereto, and serve in the corps of invalids when required, or on refusing to do so, shall be struck off the list of pensioners; unless the person so refusing have a family, or be otherwise peculiarly circumstanced, and the governor or president and the council of the State he belongs to, or in which he resides, are of opinion an exception should be made in his favour, or an exemption granted him from such service, a certificate of which opinion he shall produce, previous to receiving his pension.

"And, whereas it may happen, that many persons, maimed, or disabled as aforesaid, by reason of their falling into the hands of the enemy, the deaths of their officers and surgeons, or other accidents, may not have it in their power to procure the certificates required, by the aforementioned resolve, to entitle them to their pensions,

"*Resolved*, that in such cases application may be made to the governor or president and council of the State to which any person maimed or disabled as aforesaid belongs, or in which he resides, and upon showing to him or them satisfactory proofs, that he was maimed or disabled in the manner before mentioned, and producing his or their certificate thereof, he shall be entitled to and receive a pension in like manner as if he produced the certificates required by the said resolve."

An Act of 1802 is the first pension law which provides for the widow and children in case of the pensioner's death. This act benefitted the officers and men disabled "in the peace establishment" of the United States. The allowance was not to exceed five dollars per month,—widow and children to receive one-half the monthly payments for a period of five years—if the widow remarried or died the payment was to go to the children.

April 10, 1806, an act was passed to provide for persons disabled by wounds received in Revolution. Proofs of disability had to be shown on affidavits of the commanding officer under whom the pensioner served; the nature of the wound by affidavit of a physician in good standing and one creditable witness that the pensioner continued in service the whole period for which he volunteered. This evidence with a statement of his life and employment since the Revolution to be filed with the Secretary of War. This act provided for an increase of pension and made invalid the transfer of any part of the pension. The full pension for a commissioned officer was one-half his monthly pay—non-commissioned officers and privates at five dollars per month. Increased in 1816 to eight dollars.

The United States treasurer paid the total amount of pension money due in each State to each State through which it was distributed to the individuals.

In March, 1818, the first pension law was passed based on service. It provided that "every commissioned and non-commissioned officer, musician, and private soldier, and all officers in the hospital department and medical staff, who served in the War of the Revolution until the end thereof, or for the term of nine months, or longer, at any period of the war, on the continental establishment"; and for similar service in the navy, provided he was still a resident citizen of the United

States, should be entitled, if an officer to twenty dollars per month, others to eight dollars per month during life. The applicant was required to make a declaration, under oath, before a judge or court of record of the county, state or territory, in which he resided, or before the District Judge of the United States of his district, of the company, regiment, and line to which he belonged, the time he entered the service, and the time and manner of leaving the service.

1820, the Act was revised so that every applicant had to prove that he was absolutely dependent upon his pension and the pensions granted under Act of 1818 were suspended; he was allowed exemption on one hundred dollars personal property, his clothing and bedding, of which he was compelled to file an inventory. It was known as "The Pauper Law".

May 15, 1828, an extra Compensation Act was passed for those who had responded to emergency calls—Officers under half pay under the resolution of 1780 drew full pay and the enlisted commissioned officer, musician and private who served through the war were entitled to eighty dollars.

The first general service pension for all officers and men over 16 years of age was not voted until 1832, the service to be proven by existing muster rolls; or by the affidavit of one commissioned officer; or two comrades who served with the applicant.

June 5th, 1834, it was, *Resolved*, That the Secretary of War report to the Senate a statement showing the names of the several Pensioners who are now or may have been heretofore placed on the pension rolls; designating their rank, annual allowance, the sums received, the laws under which their pensions have been granted, and the State or Continental line in which they served, at the date when placed upon the roll, their ages, and the States and Counties in which they severally reside; also, the names of the Pension Agents who have received compensation as such, and the amount of such compensation, and the act under which it was allowed; the names of the clerks who are, and who have been employed in the Pension Office, and the sums paid them as compensation, with a statement of the aggregate sum paid in each state, and an aggregate statement of the whole sum disbursed on account of pensions. That he be also directed to report to the Senate the regulations adopted at the War Department relating to the proofs necessary to entitle claimants to the benefit of the Act of June, 1832.

Attest, Walter Lowrie, Secretary.

"The pension agents named for Territory of Michigan prior to 1834 are Thomas Rowland, Detroit, and Ellis Doty, Detroit.

(Signed) J. L. EDWARDS,
Oct. 12, 1835   Commissioner of Pensions."

Senate Documents, 23rd Congress, vols. 12–14.

Ed. note:—June 30, 1834, the Senate ordered the pension records printed and five copies transmitted to each state and filed at the "Courts of Record." March 3, 1835, the list of pensioners on file on the Treasury office rolls was ordered printed and distributed.

BOUNTY LANDS

Concerning the "bounty lands" in Michigan, for United States soldiers, the following is quoted from *Outlines of the Political History of Michigan*, by James V. Campbell.

"In 1812, May 6, among other war legislation, an act was passed setting aside two millions of acres of land in Michigan, as bounty lands for soldiers. As soon as the war was over, and circumstances permitted, Mr. Tiffin, the Surveyor General, sent agents to Michigan to select a place for locating these lands. Their report was such as to induce him to recommend the transfer of bounty locations to some other part of the United States. They began on the boundary line between Ohio and Indiana (which was the western limit of the lands surrendered to the United States by the Indian treaty of 1807) and, following it north for fifty miles, they described the country as an unbroken series of tamarack swamps, bogs and sand-barrens, with not more than one acre in a hundred, and probably not one in a thousand, fit for cultivation. Mr. Tiffin communicated this evil report to the Commissioner of the General Land Office, Josiah Meigs, and he and the Secretary of War, Mr. Crawford, secured the repeal of so much of the law as applied to Michigan. They were stimulated by a second report of the surveyors, who found the country worse and worse as they proceeded. In April, 1816, the law was changed, and lands were granted, instead, in Illinois and Missouri.

"This postponed settlements, but it saved Michigan from one of the most troublesome sources of litigation which has ever vexed any country. It was in that way a benefit. But the report of the surveyors is one of the unaccountable things of those days. Surveyors are usually good judges of land, and not likely to be deceived by the water standing on the surface of the ground, where the nature of the vegetation shows the soil cannot be marshy or sterile. A few instances have been found in our Territorial and State experiences, where surveyors made imaginary sketches of large tracts, and returned them as actual surveys, when they had never visited the places. That trick was of later invention. It may be that the surveyors did not desire to run lines which bordered on the Potawatamie country, for fear of personal risks, which were certainly possible. But the country was not unknown. It had been traversed frequently by traders and others, and was, not very long before, frequented by buffaloes in great numbers. The fact that Michigan contained so many Indians was proof that its lands were good, for they seldom congregate except in eligible regions. Mellish had published, a few years before, a very accurate general account of the whole Lower Peninsula, in which the country is as well described as it could be in as few words to-day. Some have supposed the surveyors were bribed by those who wished to prevent settlements. Although there were persons interested in that direction, there is no evidence that they interfered. It is nevertheless possible that they either bribed—or more probably adopted the cheaper course of scaring—the surveying party."

PUBLIC LANDS

"Congress in 1796, had provided for the survey and sale of the public lands in sections of six hundred and forty acres, at a minimum price of two dollars an acre, giving credit for a part of the purchase price if desired. Changes were afterwards made in the interest of purchasers with small means, and in 1817 sales in eighty-acre lots were authorized. In 1818 the surveys had so far progressed that sales were begun in Michigan. In 1820 the minimum price was reduced to one dollar twenty-five cents an acre. Ten years later preemption rights began to be given to actual settlers upon the public lands. By this legislation it was made easy for any prudent and industrious person to obtain land sufficient for moderate wants."—From Cooley's *Michigan*.

"April 23rd, 1820, Congress passed an act authorizing the sale of public lands at $1.25 per acre, full payment at purchase. 'A great event in the history of Michigan.' At the opening of the land office in Michigan, the public lands were offered at auction. Lands not 'bid off' were subject to sale thereafter at two dollars per acre, one fourth paid at time of entry, the balance in one, two, and three years, with interest. All land sold before July 3, 1820, was sold under that law.

"April 23, 1820, Congress passed an act authorizing the sale of public lands at one dollar and twenty-five cents, full payment and known as the 'ten shillings act'."—Drake's *History of Oakland County*, (1872)

PUBLIC LANDS, 1836

Land District.	Est.	Office.	Registers.	Receivers.
Detroit	1804	Detroit	Olmsted, Hugh	Kearsley, Jonathan.
Monroe	1823	Monroe	Bulkley, G. T.	Miller, D. B.
Kalamazoo	1831	Kalamazoo	Edwards, Abraham	Sheldon, Thos. C.
(First located at White Pigeon)				
Saginaw	1836	Flint	Hoffman, Michael	Hascall, Chas. C.
Grand River	1836	Ionia	Sherman, Benjamin	Richmond, Wm. A.

Ed. note:—An excellent article on changes in the county boundaries may be found in *Michigan History Magazine*, July, 1919.

PENSIONERS OF TERRITORIAL MICHIGAN

From the PENSION ESTABLISHMENT Records Published
by the War Department in 1836.

GEORGE ALFRED
Monroe County

ALFRED, George, private.
Placed on Pension Roll, July 3, 1833, at age of 70 years.
Service:—Vermont continental line.
Pension began Mar. 4, 1831.
Annual allowance $40.00. Sums received $120.00.
Inscribed under Act of Congress passed June 7, 1832.

EBENEZER ANNABLE
Cass County

ANNABLE, Ebenezer, private and sergeant.
Placed on Pension Roll, Mar. 3, 1834, at age of 76
years.
Service:—New York continental line.
Pension began Mar. 4, 1831.
Annual allowance $89.00. Sums received $267.00.
Inscribed under Act of Congress of June 7, 1832.
Remarks:—Transferred from Onondaga Co., N. Y.
Ed. note:—See also Revolutionary Soldiers buried in
Mich.

ARCHIBALD ARMSTRONG
Washtenaw County

ARMSTRONG, Archibald, private.
Placed on Pension Roll, Apr. 30, 1818, at age of 69
years.

Service:—New York continental line.
Pension began Apr. 25, 1818.
Annual allowance $96.00.   Sums received $1,474.00.
Inscribed under Act of Mar. 18, 1818.
Remarks:—Transferred from Ontario Co., N. Y.
Ed. note:—The service given in *New York in Revolution* is as follows:—"Enlisted in 1st regiment of the line under Col. Goose Van Schaick; enlisted under Col. Philip Van Cortland, 2nd reg., of the line; in the levies under Col. Albert Pawling; in Orange Co. militia, 4th regiment under Col. John Hathorn; in Tyron Co. militia, 4th regiment under Col. Peter Bellinger." See also Revolutionary Soldiers buried in Mich.

ROBERT ATKINSON
Wayne County

ATKINSON, Robert, private.
Placed on Pension Roll, Nov. 13, 1815.
Service:—3rd U. S. infantry.
Pension began Oct. 15, 1815.
Annual allowance $72.00.   Sums received $1,288.00.
Inscribed under Acts of Apr. 24, 1816.

GIDEON BADGER
Monroe County

BADGER, Gideon, private.
Placed on Pension Roll, Aug. 2, 1819, at age of 62 years.
Died Mar. 26, 1826.
Service:—Mass. continental line.
Pension began June 3, 1818.
Annual allowance $96.00.   Sums received $747.44.
Inscribed under Act of Congress passed Mar. 18, 1818.
Remarks:—Transferred to and from New York.

NATHANIEL BALDWIN
Oakland County

BALDWIN, Nathaniel, private.
Placed on Pension Roll, March 4, 1834, at the age of 74 years.
Service:—Conn. militia.
Pension began Mar. 4, 1831.
Annual allowance $20.00.   Sums received $60.00.
Inscribed under Act of June 7, 1832.
Ed. note:—See also Revolutionary Soldiers buried in Michigan.

JONATHAN BARRON
St. Clair County

BARRON, Jonathan, private.
Placed on Pension Roll, Apr. 15, 1833, at the age of 74 years.
Service:—New Hampshire continental line.
Pension began Mar. 4, 1831.
Annual allowance $57.22.   Sums received $171.66.
Inscribed under Act passed June 7, 1832.
Remarks:—Transferred from Grafton Co., N. H.
Ed. note: — See also Revolutionary Soldiers buried in Michigan.

JOSEPH BATES
Wayne County

BATES, Joseph, private.
Placed on Pension Roll, May 1, 1820, at the age of 71 years.
Service:—Conn. continental line.
Pension began July 19, 1819.
Annual allowance $96.00.
Inscribed under Act of Congress passed Mar. 18, 1818.
Ed. note:—On census roll of Detroit, 1827.

RICHARD BEAN
St. Clair County

BEAN, Richard, private.
Placed on Pension Roll, (1st) Oct. 13, 1817; (2nd) Mar.
21, 1823.
Service:—17th U. S. infantry.
Pension began June 14, 1815; increased Jan. 7, 1823.
Annual allowance $72.00; (2nd) $96.00.
Inscribed under Acts of military establishment.

JOHN BEMIS
Lenawee County

BEMIS, John, private.
Placed on Pension Roll, Oct. 21, 1828.
Died June 10, 1831.
Service:—Regulars, N. H. line.
Pension began Mar. 3, 1826.
Annual allowance $80.00.   Sums received $421.77.
Inscribed under Act of Congress passed May 15, 1828.
Remarks:—Name of agent, Wonott Lawrence.

GEORGE BEST
Wayne County

BEST, George, private.
Placed on Pension Roll, Apr. 4, 1817.
Service:—3rd U. S. infantry.
Pension began Feb. 7, 1816.
Annual allowance $72.00.   Sums received $1,229.00.
Inscribed under Acts of military establishment.

SAMUEL BLACK
Jackson County

BLACK, Samuel, private.
Placed on Pension Roll, May 2, 1833, at the age of 69.
Service:—Mass. continental line.
Pension began Mar. 4, 1831.
Annual allowance $30.80. Sums received $92.64.
Inscribed under Act of Congress passed June 7, 1832.
Remarks:—Transferred from Wayne Co., N. Y.

HENRY T. BLAKE
Wayne County

BLAKE, Henry T., musician.
Placed on Pension Roll, May 3, 1831.
Died July 7, 1832.
Service:—19th U. S. infantry.
Pension began Apr. 26, 1831.
Annual allowance $72.00. Sums received $86.20.
Inscribed under Acts of military establishment.

FREEMAN BLAKELY
Macomb County

BLAKELY, Freeman, private.
Placed on Pension Roll, Feb. 15, 1815.
Service:—31st U. S. infantry.
Pension began June 5, 1815.
Annual allowance $96.00. Sums received $1,751.68.
Inscribed under Acts of military establishment.

JOHN BLANCHARD
Oakland County

BLANCHARD, John, private.
Placed on Pension Roll, July 30, 1834, at the age of 71.
Service:—New Hampshire militia.
Pension began Mar. 4, 1831.
Annual allowance $80.00. Sums received ———.
Inscribed under Act of Congress, June 7, 1832.

LEMUEL BOLTER
Cass County

BOLTER, Lemuel, private.
Placed on Pension Roll, Sept. 24, 1825.
Service:—Mass. continental line.
Pension began Sept. 5, 1825.
Annual allowance $96.00. Sums received $720.00.
Inscribed under Act of Congress, Mar. 18, 1818.
Remarks:—Transferred from Ohio, Pittsburg, Mar. 4, 1833.

ASA BRIGGS
Kalamazoo County

BRIGGS, Asa, private and sergeant.
Placed on Pension Roll, Oct. 9, 1833, at the age of 79 years.
Service:—Vermont continental line.
Pension began Mar. 4, 1831.
Annual allowance $66.66. Sums received $166.65.
Inscribed under Act of Congress passed June 7, 1832.
Ed. note:—"Came to Mich., May, 1831, through the wilderness of Calhoun county. They had come in

the old mud wagon from Detroit to Jacksonburg and made the rest of their journey on foot. They were going by way of Tuttles to Gull Prairie. The party consisted of Joseph and Philip Corey, Cyrus Lovell, a young lawyer, and Deacons Philip Gray, Samuel Brown and Asa Briggs."

AARON BRINCK
Wayne County

BRINCK, Aaron, private.
Placed on Pension Roll, (1st) ——; (2nd) Feb. 29, 1820.
Died July 19, 1833.
Service:—Revolutionary army.
Pension began Jan. 26, 1809; increased Apr. 24, 1816.
Annual allowance (1st) $60.00; (2nd) $96.00. Sums received (1st) $434.83; (2nd) $1,654.93.
Inscribed, Apr. 27, 1810; increased, Apr. 24, 1816.
Remarks:—Transferred from N. Y.

PHINEAS BROWN
Lenawee County

BROWN, Phineas, sergeant.
Placed on Pension Roll, Aug. 9, 1833, at the age of 79.
Service:—Mass. continental line.
Pension began Mar. 4, 1831.
Annual allowance $105.00. Sums received $315.00.
Inscribed under Act of Congress passed June 7, 1832.

ALEXANDER CAMPBELL
Wayne County

CAMPBELL, Alexander, private and sergeant.
Placed on Pension Roll, (1st) Feb. 19, 1819; (2nd)—

Died Jan. 4, 1826.

Service:—5th U. S. infantry.

Pension began Jan. 18, 1818; increased Sept. 11, 1823.

Annual allowance (1st) $72.00; (2nd) $96.00. Sums received (1st) $325.38; (2nd) $222.40.

Inscribed and increased under Acts of military establishment.

Remarks:—Transferred from Massachusetts.

Ed. note:— "In 1821 settled on S. 33. T. I. N., R. 11 E. Henry Stephens, Alex. Campbell, Diadate Hubbard, Abraham Noyes, J. Goddard, Hezekiah Gridley, James Lockwood, and David Williams purchased land and were among the first settlers of Oakland county." *Mich. Hist. Colls.*, III.

NATHANIEL CASE
Wayne County

CASE, Nathaniel, captain.

Placed on Pension Roll, Apr. 1, 1834.

Service:—New York militia.

Pension began Feb. 13, 1834.

Annual allowance $240.00.

Inscribed under Acts of Apr. 24, 1816.

JAMES A. CHADWICK
Oakland County

CHADWICK, James A., corporal.

Placed on Pension Roll, Aug. 1, 1817.

Service:—4th U. S. rifles.

Pension began Nov. 29, 1814; increased Aug. 3, 1833.

Annual allowance (1st) $32.00; (2nd) $96.00. Sums received (1st) $597.68; (2nd) $8.26.

Inscribed and increased under Acts of military establishment.
Remarks:—Transferred from N. Y.

JOSHUA CHAMBERLAIN
Oakland County

CHAMBERLAIN, Joshua, private.
Placed on Pension Roll, Nov. 27, 1818, at the age of 63 years.
Service:—Revolutionary army.
Pension began Apr. 3, 1818.
Annual allowance $96.00. Sums received $808.26.
Inscribed under Act of Congress passed Mar. 18, 1818.
Remarks:—Transferred from Niagara Co., N. Y.

JAMES F. CHITTENDEN
Oakland County

CHITTENDEN, James F., private.
Placed on Pension Roll, (1st) Jan. 11, 1830; (2nd) ——.
Service:—23rd U. S. infantry.
Pension began Jan. 2, 1830; (2nd) May 17, 1832.
Annual allowance, $48.00; increased to $96.00. Sums received $114.00; $124.80.
Inscribed and increased under Acts of military establishment.
Remarks:—Transferred from Albany.
Ed. note:—On census roll of Detroit, 1827. *Mich. Hist. Colls.*, XII, 462½.

JOSEPH CLARK
Kalamazoo County

CLARK, Joseph, ensign.
Placed on Pension Roll, Apr. 24, 1832.

Service:—New York militia.
Pension began Apr. 7, 1832.
Annual allowance $78.00.   Sums received $109.84.
Inscribed, Apr. 24, 1816.
Ed. note:—(1) Lt. Joseph Clark, 76th reg., is mentioned
in a commissary bill dated Feb. 26, 1824, and again
in the *Proceedings* of the Board of Survey, July, 1822,
Canadian Archives, Ottawa, files concerning Terr.
of Mich. (2) The name of Joseph Clark occurs
with the names of enlisted men in 2nd reg., West-
chester Co. militia, N. Y., under Col. Thomas Thomas.
N. Y. in Rev., p. 207.

LEVI COLLINS
Macomb County

COLLINS, Levi, private.
Placed on Pension Roll, Nov. 30, 1810, at the age of
73.
Service:—New Hampshire continental line.
Pension began Apr. 29, 1818.
Annual allowance $96.00.   Sums received $1,425.32.
Inscribed under Act of Congress passed Mar. 18, 1818.
Remarks:—Transferred from Niagara Co., N. Y.
Ed. note:—In a report by Lt. Col. England to Lt. Gov.
Lincoe, dated Feb., 1794, is the following statement:
"Collins, who I sent you prisoner last winter, is the
principal guide to Wayne's army."   Canadian Ar-
chives concerning Terr. of Mich.

ABRAHAM COOK
Wayne County

COOK, Abraham, private.
Placed on Pension Roll, Sept. 5, 1822.

Service:—Mich. militia.

Pension began June 3, 1822; Apr. 30, 1832.

Annual allowance $48.00; $96.00. Sums received, $474.26; $33.06.

Inscribed under Acts of 1806; increased under Acts of military establishment.

Ed. note:—Name occurs on the election roll of 1799; was an inhabitant of Detroit, 1806; name on highway tax, 1812; on subscription for purchase of gun powder, 1812; farm mentioned in petition of Sept. 11, 1814, to Judge Witherell, asking a road be laid out continuing Jefferson Ave.; name on census roll of 1827; "Lived north of Jefferson Ave., (1832) in Detroit." See *Mich. Hist. Colls.*

MOSES B. COOK
"Lenawe" County

COOK, Moses B., private.

Placed on Pension Roll, Apr. 25, 1820, at the age of 73 years.

Service:—New York continental line.

Pension began June 16, 1818.

Annual allowance $96.00. Sums received $1,460.08.

Inscribed under Act of Congress passed Mar. 18, 1818.

Remarks:—Transferred to and from Albany.

Ed. note:—*New York in Revolution* gives Moses Cook, Sr., and Moses Cook, Jr., in the 3rd regiment, Dutchess Co. militia, under Col. John Field; also, a Moses Cook as an enlisted man in 4th regiment, N. Y. continental line, under Col. James Holmes.

DAVID A. CORYELL
Washtenaw County

CORYELL, David A., private.
Placed on Pension Roll, Aug. 9, 1833, at the age of 76 years.
Service:—New Jersey continental line.
Pension began Mar. 4, 1831.
Annual allowance $80.00.   Sums received $240.00.
Inscribed under Act of Congress passed June 7, 1832.

HENRY CREMER
Wayne County

CREMER, Henry, private.
Placed on Pension Roll, May 3, 1816.
Died May 20, 1830.
Service:—In 29th U. S. infantry.
Pension began July 1, 1815.
Inscribed under Acts of military establishment.
Remarks:—Transferred from New York.

JOTHAM CURTISS
Washtenaw County

CURTISS, Jotham, private.
Placed on Pension Roll, June 6, 1828.
Service:—Connecticut continental line.
Pension began May 21, 1828.
Annual allowance $96.00.   Sums received $459.72.
Inscribed under Act of Congress passed Mar. 18, 1818.
Remarks:—Transferred from Medina Co., Ohio.

EPHRAIM DAINS
Wayne County

DAINS, Ephraim, private.
Placed on Pension Roll, July 16, 1819, at the age of 73.
Service:—Connecticut continental line.
Pension began May 26, 1818.
Annual allowance $96.00.   Sums received $1,474.40.
Inscribed under Act of Congress passed Mar. 18, 1818.
Remarks:—Transferred from Ontario Co., N. Y.

JOSEPH DARLING
Jackson County

DARLING, Joseph, private.
Placed on Pension Roll, Jan. 3, 1833, at the age of 70
years.
Service:—Massachusetts continental line.
Pension began Mar. 4, 1831.
Annual allowance $20.00.   Sums received $60.00.
Inscribed under Act of Congress passed June 7, 1832.
Ed. note:—"On Ganson St., northeast of the village
of Jacksonburg were (in 1835) Constant McGuire
and sons and Joseph Darling and sons". See also
Revolutionary Soldiers Buried in Mich. Name of
Joseph Darling on the list of men who served in
Revolution from New Haven, Conn.

JONATHAN DEAR
Wayne County

DEAR, Jonathan, private.
Placed on Pension Roll, Apr. 23, 1819, at the age of 72
years.
Service:—Connecticut continental line.

Pension began Apr. 8, 1818.

Annual allowance $96.00. Sums received $1,492.92.

Inscribed under Act of Congress passed Mar. 18, 1818.

Remarks:—Transferred from Jefferson Co., N. Y.

Ed. note:—The name of a Jonathan Deare occurs on
New Jersey Roll of officers and men in Revolutionary
war. "A 1st major, 1st reg., of Middlesex; lieut.
colonel from Middlesex, July 25, 1776; resigned Mar.
31, 1778; elected collector of customs, eastern district,
N. J., Dec. 12, 1778."

STEPHEN DOWNING
Monroe County

DOWNING, Stephen, private.

Placed on Pension Roll, Oct. 9, 1833, at the age of 72
years.

Service in Connecticut continental line.

Pension began Mar. 4, 1831.

Annual allowance $70.00. Sums received $210.00.

Inscribed under Act of Congress passed June 7, 1832.

Data recorded by Mrs. Eli Cupp, chapter historian,
Abiel Fellows chapter, *D. A. R. M. S. Colls. E.*

Ed. note:—"Stephen Downing was born Feb. 12, 1762;
married Susannah Helm, born Sept. 16, 1767. To
them were born ten children. Their son Rufus
Downing was born Aug. 22, 1792; married Lola
Weston, Feb. 16, 1816. Children of Rufus and Lola
Downing were:—Lola; Jane; Zelia, b. 1819; Helms;
Lewis; Theodore; Edwin; Susannah; Sample; and
Celia. Living descendants: —1918, Drs. Alfred and
Franklin Wade. Family Bible record in the possession
of Mrs. Celia Howes, a great-granddaughter of
Stephen Downing. Rufus Downing conducted a trad-
ing post located on S. E. corner of E. ½ of S. E. ¼ S. 9,

T. 6, S. of R. 10 W. Nottawa Twp. St. Joseph Co.,
Michigan. The land on which the trading post was located was entered from the Government by Lindsey
Warfield of Gates Co., N. Y., June 7, 1831; Warfield
deeded one acre to School District No. 1 of Nottawa.
The trading post was located between the school house
and the corner of the Section on the old trail, afterwards a branch of the old Territorial road." The
probate records of St. Joseph Co. give inventories of
the personal property and real estate of Rufus Downing who died Sept. 1, 1834. The trading post was
marked by the Abiel Fellows chapter, D. A. R. of
Three Rivers, Michigan, September 17, 1918.

MARTIN DUBOIS
Washtenaw County

DuBois, Martin, private.
Placed on Pension Roll, Aug. 9, 1833, at the age of 70
years.
Service:—New York continental line.
Pension began Mar. 4, 1831.
Annual allowance $30.00. Sums received $90.00.
Inscribed under Act of Congress passed June 7, 1832.
Ed. note:—See also Revolutionary Soldiers Buried in
Mich. *N. Y. in Revolution*, p. 71, lists Martin
DuBois, 1777, with the levies (N. Y.), under Col.
Frederick Weissenfels.

WILLIAM DUNBAR
Wayne County

Dunbar, William, private.
Placed on Pension Roll, June 19, 1819, at the age of 60
years.

Service in New York continental line.
Pension began Feb. 17, 1819.
Annual allowance $96.00.   Sums received $388.00.
Inscribed under Act of Congress passed Mar. 18, 1818.
Ed. note:—*N. Y. in Revolution*, pp. 32, 49, 78, 83, 108,
    221, gives the following service:—"William Dunbar in
    2nd reg. of the line, under Col. Philip Van Cortland;
    4th reg. of enlisted men in N. Y. line; in the levies
    under Col. Lewis DuBois; in levies under Col. Albert
    Pawling; in Albany county militia, 6th reg., under
    Col. Stephen John Schuylar and on the Land Bounty
    Rights list for Albany Co. militia, 1st regiment."

BENJAMIN ELLSWORTH
Wayne County

ELLSWORTH, Benjamin, private.
Placed on Pension Roll, June 7, 1833, at the age of 80
    years.
Service:—New York militia.
Pension began Mar. 4, 1831.
Annual allowance $24.98.   Sums received $74.94.
Inscribed under Act of Congress passed June 7, 1832.
Remarks:—Transferred from Seneca Co., N. Y.
Ed. note:—*N. Y. in Revolution*, p. 196, gives service of
    Benj. Ellsworth, in the 3rd reg. of Ulster Co. (N. Y.)
    militia under Col. Levi Pawling.

ABIEL FELLOWS
Kalamazoo County

FELLOWS, Abiel, private.
Placed on Pension Roll, Sept. 25, 1833, at the age of
    70 years.
Service:—Connecticut continental line,

Pension began Mar. 4, 1831.
Annual allowance $70.00.   Sums received $210.00.
Inscribed under Act of Congress passed June 7, 1832.
Ed. note:—See also Revolutionary Soldiers Buried in
Mich.

THOMAS FERGO
St. Clair County

FERGO, Thomas, private.
Placed on Pension Roll, Nov. 10, 1832, at the age of
77 years.
Service:—Connecticut continental line.
Pension began Mar. 4, 1831.
Annual allowance $40.00.   Sums received $120.00.
Inscribed under Act of Congress passed June 7, 1832.

RICHARD FERGUSON
Oakland County

FERGUSON, Richard, private.
Placed on Pension Roll, Apr. 28, 1832.
Service:—3rd U. S. artillery.
Pension began Dec. 26, 1826.
Annual allowance $48.00.   Sums received $321.20.
Inscribed under Acts of military establishment.

JABEZ FISK
"Lenawe" County

FISK, Jabez, private.
Placed on Pension Roll, May 31, 1817.
Service:—New York volunteers.
Pension began (1st) Nov. 9, 1814; (2nd) Apr. 24, 1816;
(3rd) Sept. 9, 1822.

Annual allowance:—(1st) $48.80; (2nd) $76.80; (3rd) $96.00. Sums received: (1st) $70.00; (2nd) $489.60; (3rd) $1,102.66.

Inscribed and increased under Acts of military establishment, Apr. 24, 1816.

Remarks:—Transferred from N. Y.

THOMAS FITZGERALD
Berrien County

FITZGERALD, Thomas, corporal.

Placed on Pension Roll, Dec. 14, 1815.

Service:—5th U. S. infantry.

Pension began (1st) June 14, 1815; (2nd) Apr. 24, 1816; (3rd) Sept. 15, 1821.

Annual allowance:—(1st) $30.00; (2nd) $48.00; (3rd) $96.00. Sums received (1st) $25.83; (2nd) $306.00; (3rd) $1,097.33.

Inscribed under Acts of military establishment, Apr. 24, 1816.

Remarks:—Transferred from N. Y., and from Indiana.

Ed. note:—Thomas Fitzgerald, mentioned by Hon. Michael Shoemaker in an address, as one of the great men who shaped the destiny of Mich., was candidate for lieutenant governor, 1839, and elected U. S. senator 1848–49.

JOHN FRANCISCO
Monroe County

FRANCISCO, John, private.

Placed on Pension Roll, Feb. 3, 1830.

Service:—N. Y. militia.

Pension began (1st) Jan. 22, 1830; (2nd) Oct. 4, 1833.

Annual allowance:—(1st) $48.00; (2nd) $72.00. Sums received, (1st) $173.73; (2nd) $30.00.

Inscribed under Acts of military establishment.
Remarks:—Transferred from N. Y.
Ed. note:—*N. Y. in Revolution* by J. A. Roberts, comptroller, gives service on pp. 32, 126, as a private in 2nd reg. N. Y. continental line under Col. Philip Van Cortland, also under Col. John Knickerbacker, in Albany Co. militia.

DANIEL FRENCH
Washtenaw County

FRENCH, Daniel, private.
Placed on Pension Roll, Feb. 20, 1816.
Service:—11th U. S. infantry.
Pension began Apr. 4, 1815.
Annual allowance $96.00. Sums received $1,768.00.
Inscribed under Acts of military establishment.
Remarks:—Transferred from Pennsylvania.
Ed. note:—On the Class Roll of Capt. Geo. Enslo's company, Province, county of Bedford, Pa., militia, the name of a Daniel French occurs in the second class for 1781. *Pa. Archives*, 5th series, V. 92.

ASA GILLETT
Washtenaw County

GILLETT, Asa, private in dragoons.
Placed on Pension Roll, May 29, 1818.
Service in Connecticut continental line.
Pension began Apr. 27, 1818.
Annual allowance $96.00. Sums received $1,425.32.
Inscribed under Act of Congress passed Mar. 18, 1818.
Remarks:—Transferred from Otsego Co., N. Y.

FRANCIS GOWEN
Wayne County

GOWEN, Francis, private.
Placed on Pension Roll, Apr. 11, 1833, at the age ot 75.
Service:—Pennsylvania continental line.
Pension began July 20, 1819.
Annual allowance $96.00.   Sums received $1,425.33.
Inscribed under Act of Congress passed Mar. 18, 1818.

BENJAMIN GRACE
Oakland County

GRACE, Benjamin, private.
Placed on Pension Roll, Apr. 13, 1819.
Service:—New Hampshire continental line.
Pension began Apr. 29, 1818.
Annual allowance $96.00.   Sums received $1,437.33.
Inscribed under Act of Congress passed Mar. 18, 1818.
Remarks:—Transferred from N. Y.

JAMES GRAHAM
Oakland County

GRAHAM, James, corporal.
Placed on Pension Roll, Aug. 9, 1833, at the age of 79
   yrs.
Service:—Pennsylvania continental line.
Pension began Mar. 4, 1831.
Annual allowance $44.00.   Sums received $132.00.
Inscribed under Act of Congress passed June 7, 1832.
Ed. note:—James and Alexander Graham were first
   settlers of Avon Twp., Oakland Co., Mich. See
   also Revolutionary Soldiers Buried in Mich.

SAMUEL GRAY
Wayne County

GRAY, Samuel, private.
Placed on Pension Roll, Jan. 11, 1816.
Died Sept. 24, 1819.
Service in New York militia.
Pension began Dec. 1, 1813; Apr. 24, 1816.
Annual allowance $40.00; $64.00.   Sums received
  $295.88; $281.81.
Inscribed and increased under Acts of military estab-
  lishment Apr. 24, 1816.
Remarks:—Transferred from New York.
Ed. note:—*N. Y. in Revolution* gives the following
  service (see pp. 50, 56, 140, 176): Private in 4th
  reg., N. Y. cont'l line under Col. James Holmes;
  private in 5th reg. of N. Y. cont'l line under Col.
  Lewis DuBois; in 3rd reg., of Dutchess Co., under
  Col. John Field; and in 2nd reg., of Tryon militia,
  under Col. Jacob Klocke.

WILLIAM GRIFFITH
"Erie" County

GRIFFITH, William, first lieutenant.
Placed on Pension Roll, Apr. 3, 1818.
Service:—Kentucky volunteers.
Pension began Nov. 20, 1813.
Annual allowance $102.00.   Sums received $1,151.88.
Inscribed under Act passed Apr. 24, 1816.
Ed. note: —Name on "Lister's returns for the tax of
  1802 for Sargent Twp., Wayne Co., U. S. Northwest
  of the Ohio River."—*Mich. Hist. Colls.*

ASAHEL HASKINS
Macomb County

HASKINS, Asahel, private.
Placed on Pension Roll, Oct. 17, 1822, at age of 70 yrs
Service:—Massachusetts continental line.
Pension began Oct. 3, 1820.
Annual allowance $96.00.   Sums received $1,240.26.
Inscribed under Act of Congress passed Mar. 18, 1818.
Remarks:—Transferred from Crawford Co., Ill.

JOHN HEATON
Wayne County

HEATON, John, private.
Placed on Pension Roll, Jan. 2, 1818.
Service:—3rd U. S. infantry.
Pension began Nov. 25, 1817.
Annual allowance $96.00.   Sums received $1,083.72.
Inscribed under Acts of military establishment.

JOSEPH HOLLAND
Macomb County

HOLLAND, Joseph, private.
Placed on Pension Roll, Feb. 4, 1834, at age of 74 yrs.
Service:—Connecticut militia.
Pension began Mar. 4, 1831.
Annual allowance $50.00.   Sums received $150.00.
Inscribed under Act of Congress passed June 7, 1832.

GEORGE HORTON
Wayne County

HORTON, George, private.
Placed on Pension Roll, Dec. 15, 1832, at age of 73 yrs.

Service:—Pennsylvania continental line.
Pension began Mar. 4, 1831.
Annual allowance $80.00.   Sums received $240.00.
Inscribed under Act of Congress passed June 7, 1832.
Remarks:—Transferred from Tioga Co., N. Y.
Ed. note:—"1782 was in class 2, 7th co., commanded by
    Capt. Henry Shoemaker, 5th battalion, Northampton
    Co, militia."   *Pa. Archives*, 5th series, VIII, 417,

JEDEDIAH HUNT
Wayne County

HUNT, Jedediah, captain.
Placed on Pension Roll, Oct. 2, 1830.
Service:—New York volunteers.
Pension began Sept. 29, 1830.
Annual allowance $240.00.   Sums received $703.20.
Inscribed under the law of Apr. 24, 1816.
Transferred to Michigan from New York.
Ed. note:—Capt. Jedediah Hunt was a passenger on
    the last trip of "Walk-In-The-Water" (1821), the
    first steam boat on the upper lakes.   *Mich. Hist.
    Colls.*

MEDE HURD
St. Joseph County

HURD, Mede, private.
Placed on Pension Roll, Aug. 10, 1832, at the age of
    77 yrs.
Service:—Connecticut continental line.
Pension began March 4, 1831.
Annual allowance $66.66.   Sums received $1,991.98.
Inscribed under Act of Congress passed June 7, 1832.
Transferred from Ulster Co., N. Y.

LEWIS JACOBS
Monroe County

JACOBS, Lewis, private.
Placed on Pension Roll, (1st) Feb. 10, 1823; (2nd) Sept. 13, 1832.
Service:—Michigan volunteers.
Pension began (1st) Dec. 16, 1822; (2nd) Sept. 5th, 1832.
Annual allowance $48.00; $96.00.   Sums received $466.65; $48.00.
Inscribed and increased under Acts of military establishment.

OLIVER JENKS
Oakland County

JENKS, Oliver, private.
Placed on Pension Roll, Sept. 8, 1818.
Service:—27th U. S. infantry.
Pension began Sept. 4, 1818.
Annual allowance $72.00.   Sums received $828.00.
Inscribed under Acts of military establishment.
Transferred from New York to Huron Co.

THOMAS JOHNSON
Wayne County

JOHNSON, Thomas, sergeant.
Placed on Pension Roll, June 25, 1833.
Service:—2nd U. S. infantry.
Pension began Oct. 21, 1832.
Annual allowance $72.00.   Sums received $62.00.
Inscribed under Acts of military establishment.

JONATHAN KEARSLEY
Wayne County

KEARSLEY, Jonathan, major.
Placed on Pension Roll, Jan. 17, 1816.
Service:—4th U. S. rifles.
Pension began June 16, 1815.
Annual allowance $360.00. Sums received $6,558.00.
Inscribed under Acts of military establishment.
Transferred from Pennsylvania to Michigan Territory.
Ed. note:—The *Mich. Hist. Colls.* are rich in anecdote
  concerning Major Kearsley, as a member of the
  Board of Regents of the University of Michigan, and
  as a receiver of public land. Feb. 25, 1825, Jonathan
  Kearsley purchased land in Shelby Twp., Macomb
  Co.; in 1832 owned property in Detroit. A tribu-
  tary of the Flint River is named for him.

BENJAMIN KNAPP
Wayne County

KNAPP, Benjamin, private.
Placed on the Pension Roll, July 12, 1823, at the age
  of 76.
Died May 10, 1833.
Service:—New York continental line.
Pension began June 1, 1823.
Annual allowance $96.00. Sums received $954.40.
Inscribed under Act of Congress, March 18, 1818.
Ed. note:—The name of Benj. Knapp occurs on the
  census roll of Detroit, 1827. In 1791 the name
  occurs on a list of discharged rangers and loyalists,
  issued to Gov. Gen. of Quebec.—A member of Col.
  Butler's rangers. *New York in the Revolution*, **pp.**

34, 43, 151, gives the following service for Private Benjamin Knapp: in 2nd regiment, New York line, under Col. Philip Van Cortland; in 3rd regiment, New York continental line, under Col. James Clutton; also, Dutchess Co. militia, 7th regiment.

NATHANIEL LANDON
Oakland County

LANDON, Nathaniel, private.
Placed on Pension Roll, Feb. 10, 1834, at the age of 77 years.
Service:—New Jersey militia.
Pension began Mar. 4, 1831.
Annual allowance $43.33.   Sums received $129.99.
Inscribed under Act of Congress passed June 7, 1832.

WILLIAM LETTS
Macomb County

LETTS, William, private.
Placed on Pension Roll, Jan. 10, 1817.
Service:—24th U. S. infantry.
Pension began Sept. 27, 1815.
Annual allowance $48.40.   Sums received $496.73.
Inscribed under Acts of military establishment.

EDWARD LOCKE
St. Clair County

LOCKE, Edward, private.
Placed on Pension Roll, Jan. 22, 1834.
Service:—5th U. S. infantry.
Pension began Apr. 25, 1833.

Annual allowance $96.00.
Inscribed under Acts of military establishment.

PETER LOWN
Wayne County

LOWN, Peter, private.
Placed on Pension Roll, Feb. 4, 1834, at the age of 74
  years.
Service:—New York militia.
Pension began Mar. 4, 1831.
Annual allowance $23.33.   Sums received $69.99.
Inscribed under Act of Congress passed June 7, 1832.

WILLIAM M'COSKEY
Wayne County

McCOSKEY, William, sur. mate.
Placed on Pension Roll, Mar. 30, 1831; commencement
  of pay, Mar. 3, 1826.
Died May 16, 1830.
Service:—Pennsylvania artillery.
Annual allowance $480.00.   Sums received $2,498.66.
Inscribed under Act of Congress passed May 15, 1828.
Remarks:—David Beard, ag't; Felicity McCoskey,
  widow.
Ed. note:—A surgeon in Gen. Wayne's army. In
  "Recollections of Early Detroit", Robert E. Roberts
  writes, "On reaching the road via Randolph St.,
  the residence was passed of the venerable medical
  gentleman of olden time, Dr. McCoskey, surgeon of
  Wayne's army, where he resided from 1796 until his
  death about 1830." "Name on census, of Detroit,
  1806; and occurs on subscription for gunpowder; also
  on the highway tax of 1812." *Mich. Hist. Colls.*

SAMUEL M'CREA
Wayne County

McCREA, Samuel, private.
Placed on Pension Roll, Nov. 20, 1819.
Died June 4, 1821.
Service:—5th U. S. infantry.
Pension began May 1, 1819.
Annual allowance $72.00.   Sums received $150.60.
Inscribed under Acts of Apr. 24, 1816.

SAMUEL M'KEE
Wayne County

McKEE, Samuel, private.
Placed on Pension Roll, Jan. 28, 1823.
Service:—3rd U. S. rifles.
Pension began (1st) Oct. 30, 1822; (2nd) Mar. 24, 1832.
Annual allowance $32.00; $96.00.   Sums received
$300.88; $138.66.
Inscribed and increased under Acts of military estab-
lishment, Apr. 25, 1808.

JOHN M'NAIR
"Iowa" County

McNAIR, John, sergeant.
Placed on Pension Roll, Mar. 10, 1834.
Service:—Mich. militia.
Pension began Mar. 8, 1834.
Annual allowance $72.00.
Inscribed under Acts of Apr. 24, 1816.

WILLIAM MAPLES
"Lenawe" County

MAPLES, William, private.
Placed on Pension Roll, Oct. 3, 1833, at age of 74 yrs.
Service:—Connecticut continental line.
Pension began Mar. 4, 1831.
Annual allowance $23.33.   Sums received $69.99.
Inscribed under Act of Congress passed June 7, 1832.

JOHN MARTIN
Wayne County

MARTIN, John, captain.
Placed on Pension Roll, Sept. 22, 1830.
Service:—New York volunteers.
Pension began Sept. 21, 1830.
Annual allowance $120.00.   Sums received $345.33.
Inscribed under Acts of Apr. 24, 1816.
Ed. note:—A John Martin was interpreter; also, Indian
   storekeeper on Island of St. Joseph, 1802.   Revolu-
   tionary service of John Martin recorded in *New York
   in Revolution*, pp. 4, 24, 63, 133, 147, 193, 254, refers
   to a private by that name.   A Lt. John Martin (*N.
   Y. in Revolution*, p. 133) was in Charlotte Co. militia
   of N. Y. under Col. John Williams.

HENRY MASSEY
Cass County

MASSEY, Henry, private.
Placed on Pension Roll, Sept. 21, 1818.
Service:—Maryland continental line.
Pension began Apr. 5, 1818.

Annual allowance $96.00. Sums received $1,479.72.
Inscribed under Act of Congress passed Mar. 18, 1818.
Remarks:—Transferred from Baltimore Co., Maryland.

ELIJAH MEASURELL
Oakland County

MEASURELL, Elijah, private.
Placed on Pension Roll, Apr. 28, 1830.
Service:—2nd U. S. infantry.
Pension began Apr. 9, 1830.
Annual allowance $72.00. Sums received $245.00.
Inscribed under Acts of military establishment.
Remarks:—Transferred from New York.

THOMPSON MAXWELL
Wayne County

MAXWELL, Thompson, private.
Placed on Pension Roll, Oct. 9, 1818, at the age of 90
 yrs.
Died Oct. 24, 1832.
Service:—New Hampshire continental line.
Pension began July 1, 1818.
Annual allowance $240.00. Sums received $3,435.33.
Inscribed under Act of Congress passed Mar. 18, 1818.
Ed. note:—The *Mich. Hist. Colls.* have many articles
 on this revolutionary soldier. Rev. E. H. Pilcher
 records Maxwell's marriage to the mother of Rev.
 Joseph Hickox; his residence sixteen miles from
 Detroit; death occurred about 1831 (which according
 to pension record would be at the age of 103). Rev.
 Pilcher gives the age as *97* and claims Maxwell's
 birth occurred in *1734*; also records that Major Max-

well was one of the "Boston tea party" in 1773, and
fought in twenty-three battles of the revolution.   In
the war of 1812 was made major in regular army.
"Spent last years in quiet retirement . . . His
dust sleeps in a country church yard, grave unmarked,
and no other record of his life than this account."
Mich. Hist. Colls. Francis Parkman refers to Maxwell as an English provincial and a pretender; to
have been a soldier under Gladwyn and discredits
the paper "Pontiac's Incursions". "The period of
service of the Rangers having expired, Major Maxwell, in Oct., 1763, returned to Mass., married and
settled in New Hampshire and resided in that
state until the Revolution, when he left a wife and
five children . . . for renewed hardships and
privation of public service". Maxwell's account of
the incursions of Chieftain Pontiac in the *Mich.
Hist. Colls.*, VIII, 364. A "Major Maxwell, commandant of the Fort (Detroit) taken prisoner by
Pontiac in 1763 and held as hostage, was tortured,
killed, on bridge of Bloody Run, and buried near the
residence of Judge Witherell, later removed to the
citadel and buried beside three pear trees." Chas.
Gouin in *Mich. Hist. Colls.*, VIII, 344. "Maxwell,
Thompson, (N. H.) 2nd Lieutenant of 3rd N. H.,
23rd May to Dec., 1775; 2nd Lieut., 2nd Continental
infantry, 1st Jan. to 31st Dec., 1776. (Died 1825)."
Heitman's *Historical Register, Officers of Continental
Army.*

FREDERICK MILLER
Wayne County

MILLER, Frederick, private.
Placed on Pension Roll, Nov. 13, 1819.
Died July 24, 1820.

Service:—5th U. S. infantry.
Pension began Apr. 29, 1819.
Annual allowance $96.00.   Sums received ————— .
Inscribed under Acts of military establishment.
Remarks:—Paid at Albany.

JONATHAN MILLER
Wayne County

MILLER, Jonathan, private.
Placed on Pension Roll, Sept. 4, 1829.
Service:—Col. Willy's reg.
Pension began Mar. 3, 1826.
Annual allowance $80.00.   Sums received $680.00.
Inscribed under Act of Congress passed May 15, 1828.
Remarks:—B. F. H. Witherell, agent.

MILES S. MILLER
Wayne County

MILLER, Miles S., private.
Placed on Pension Roll, Feb. 18, 1817.
Died Aug. 12, 1821.
Service:—2nd U. S. light dragoons.
Pension began May 2, 1815.
Annual allowance $96.00.   Sums received $602.66.
Inscribed under Acts of military establishment.

HENRY MEYERS
Wayne County

MEYERS, Henry, private.
Placed on Pension Roll, May 22, 1823.
Service:—New York volunteers.
Pension began Mar. 29, 1823.

Annual allowance $72.00.   Sums received $607.20.

Inscribed under Acts of military establishment.

Remarks:—Transferred from New York.

Ed. note:—A Henry Meyer is registered on p. 108 of
N. Y. in Revolution: Sixth reg., Albany Co. militia
under Col. Stephen John Schuyler.

THOMAS NELSON
"Lenawe" County

NELSON, Thomas, private.

Placed on Pension Roll, Mar. 3, 1834, at the age of 77
years.

Service:—Vermont militia.

Pension began Mar. 4, 1831.

Annual allowance $26.66.   Sums received $79.98.

Inscribed under Act of Congress passed June 7, 1832.

Ed. note:—Name is on the pay-roll of Lt. Moses Johnson's Co., in Col. Wm. William's regiment Sept. 25
to Oct. 17, 1777, 24 days service, am't due ———
Vermont Revolutionary Rolls, p. 41.

ANDREW NICHOLS
Washtenaw County

NICHOLS, Andrew, private.

Placed on Pension Roll, Dec. 10, 1825, at the age of
74 yrs.

Service:—New Hampshire continental line.

Pension began Nov. 21, 1825.

Annual allowance $96.00.   Sums received $749.44.

Inscribed under Act of Congress passed Mar. 18, 1818.

Remarks:—Transferred from St. Lawrence Co., N. Y.

Ed. note:—1834, Andrew Nichols located in Commerce,
Oakland Co.

JOSEPH G. ODALL
Wayne County

ODALL, Joseph G., ensign.
Placed on Pension Roll, Nov. 4, 1833.
Service:—New York volunteers.
Pension began Sept. 30, 1833.
Annual allowance $120.00.
Inscribed under Acts of Apr. 24, 1816.

DANIEL OLDS
Lenawee County

OLDS, Daniel, private and sergeant.
Placed on Pension Roll, Sept. 25, 1833, at the age of
   75 years.
Service:—Connecticut continental line.
Pension began Mar. 4, 1831.
Annual allowance $106.66.   Sums received $266.65.
Inscribed under Act of Congress passed June 7, 1832.

WILLIAM OLDS
Macomb County

OLDS, William, private.
Placed on Pension Roll, Sept. 19, 1825.
Service:—Michigan militia.
Pension began Jan. 27, 1825.
Annual allowance $32.00.   Sums received $198.13.
Inscribed under Acts of military establishment.
Remarks:—Transferred from N. Y.

ADAM OVERROCKER
Washtenaw County

OVERROCKER, Adam, private.
Placed on Pension Roll, Aug. 9, 1833, at age of 73 yrs.
Service:—New York continental line.
Pension began Mar. 4, 1831.
Annual allowance $80.00.   Sums received $240.00.
Inscribed under Act of Congress passed June 7, 1832.
Ed. note:—Service is given in N. Y. in Revolution, p.
127, as: "Enlisted, Albany Co. militia, 4th. regi-
ment, under Col. John Knickerbacker."

WILLIAM PANGBURN
Wayne County

PANGBURN, William, private.
Placed on Pension Roll, Nov. 30, 1821, at age of 75
yrs.
Service:—N. Y. continental line.
Pension began Jan. 8, 1821.
Annual allowance $96.00.   Sums received $1,079.20.
Inscribed under Act of Congress passed Mar. 18, 1818.
Ed. note:—Service in Revolutionary war is given in
N. Y. in Revolution, pp. 52, 107, 224: "Enlisted 4th
regiment of N. Y. continental line; in 5th regiment,
Albany Co. militia, under Col. Garritt G. Van
Bergh.   Entered, also, with the names of 3rd reg.,
Albany Co. militia, entitled to land bounty rights."
See also Revolutionary Soldiers Buried in Mich.

PAUL PARCELS
Wayne County

PARCELS (Purcels), Paul, private.
Placed on Pension Roll, Apr. 24, 1818.

Died May 1, 1818.
Service:—5th U. S. infantry.
Pension began June 2, 1817.
Annual allowance $64.00.   Sums received $58.46.
Inscribed under Acts of military establishment.

ROBERT PARKER
Wayne County

PARKER, Robert, private.
Placed on Pension Roll, Sept. 22, 1818, at the age of
    74 yrs.
Service:—Massachusetts continental line.
Pension began Apr. 6, 1818.
Annual allowance $96.00.   Sums received $1,479.73.
Inscribed under Act of Congress passed Mar. 18, 1818.
Remarks:—Transferred from Clinton Co., N. Y.

WILLIAM PATEE
Wayne County

PATEE, William, private.
Placed on Pension Roll, Feb. 9, 1834, at the age of 79
    yrs.
Service:—New Hampshire continental line.
Pension began Mar. 4, 1831.
Annual allowance $60.00.   Sums received $180.00.
Inscribed under Act of Congress passed June 7, 1832.

JOHN PETTIGREW
Cass County

PETTIGREW, John, private.
Placed on Pension Roll, Mar. 4, 1834, at age of 76 yrs.
Service:—Pennsylvania continental line.

Pension began Mar. 4, 1831.

Annual allowance $40.00.   Sums received $120.00.

Inscribed under Act of Congress passed June 7, 1832.

Ed. note:—"In 2nd class, 3rd co., 9th battalion, Pa. militia."   *Pa. Archives*, 5th series, VII, 908.

Name also on "A return of the 4th co., 6th battalion of Lancaster Co., Pennsylvania, 1778–'9."   "John Pettycrew, 2nd class, under Capt. James McCreight served at Northumberland."   *Pa. Arch.*, 5th series, VII, 548.   See also Revolutionary Soldiers Buried in Michigan.

NATHAN PUFFER
Mackinac County

PUFFER, Nathan, private.

Placed on Pension Roll, Mar. 25, 1823.

Service:—U. S. army.

Pension began May 7, 1821.

Annual allowance $96.00.   Sums received $1,183.44.

Inscribed under Acts of military establishment.

JAMES RANDALL
Wayne County

RANDALL, James, private.

Placed on Pension Roll, (1st) June 28, 1824; (2nd) Mar. 4, 1826; (3rd) July 1, 1830.

Service:—2nd U. S. artillery.

Annual allowance $72.00; $48.00; $72.00.   Sums received $151.40; $204.26; $228.60.

Inscribed under Acts military establishment.

Ed. note:—*Early History of Macomb County*, by Warren Parker, mentions James Randall among the men who began life in the wilderness, developed its resources, and contributed to the wealth and prosperity of Macomb Co. *Mich. Hist. Colls.*, XVIII, 502.

JACOB RATTANEUR
Wayne County

RATTANEUR, Jacob, private.
Placed on Pension Roll, (1st) July 1, 1830; (2nd) Apr. 2, 1824.
Service:—New York militia.
Pension began (1st) Mar. 4, 1789; (2nd) Apr. 24, 1816.
Annual allowance $60.00; $96.00.   Sums received $1,628.33; $1,714.66.
Inscribed and increased under Acts of Sept. 29, 1789 and Apr. 24, 1816.
Remarks:—Transferred from New York.

JOHN REYNOLDS
Mackinac County

REYNOLDS, John, private.
Placed on Pension Roll, Mar. 25, 1823.
Service:—U. S. army.
Pension began (1st) July 13, 1810; increased Apr. 24, 1816.
Annual allowance (1st) $36.00; (2nd) $57.00. Sums received $243.10.
Inscribed under Acts of July 5, 1812; increased under Act of Apr. 24, 1816.

AMOS RICHARDS
Cass County

RICHARDS, Amos, private.
Placed on Pension Roll, Dec. 25, 1821, at the age of 77 years.

Service:—Connecticut continental line.
Pension began Apr. 8, 1818.
Annual allowance $96.00.   Sums received $1,430.92.
Inscribed under Act of Congress passed Mar. 18, 1818.
Remarks:—Transferred from Jefferson Co., N. Y.

LEVI ROSS
Wayne County

Ross, Levi, private.
Placed on Pension Roll, Oct. 1, 1818, at age of 85 yrs.
Service:—New Jersey continental line.
Pension began May 7, 1818.
Annual allowance $96.00.   Sums received $1,422.44.
Inscribed under Act of Congress passed Mar. 18, 1818.
Remarks:—Transferred from Seneca Co., N. Y.

JOHN L. SHEAR
Wayne County

SHEAR, John L., private.
Placed on Pension Roll, June 18, 1817.
Service:—New York militia.
Pension began Nov. 1, 1812.
Annual allowance $48.00.   Sums received $996.00.
Inscribed under Act of Apr. 24, 1816.
Remarks:—Transferred from N. Y.

ISAAC W. SHUMAWAY
"Lenawe" County

SHUMAWAY, Isaac W., private.
Placed on Pension Roll, July 23, 1819, at the age of
73 yrs.

Service:—Massachusetts continental line.
Pension began Apr. 21, 1818.
Annual allowance $96.00. Sums received $1,475.55.
Inscribed under Act of Congress passed Mar. 18, 1818.
Remarks:—Transferred from Ontario Co., N. Y.

JOHN SILSBEE
Cass County

SILSBEE, John, Captain.
Placed on Pension Roll, Feb. 6, 1817.
Service:—New York militia.
Pension began Feb. 11, 1814; increased Apr. 24, 1816.
Annual allowance (1st) $180.00; (2nd) increased to
$240.00.   Sums received (1st) $396.00; (2nd)
$4,286.33.
Inscribed and increased (1st) under Acts of military
establishment; (2nd) Apr. 24, 1816.
Remarks:—Transferred from Albany.

DARIUS SMEAD
Wayne County

SMEAD, Darius, private.
Placed on Pension Roll, Mar. 25, 1819, at the age of
68 yrs.
Service:—New Hampshire continental line.
Pension began Apr. 6, 1818.
Annual allowance $96.00. Sums received $1,522.66.
Inscribed under Act of Congress passed Mar. 18, 1818.
Remarks:—Transferred from Seneca Co., N. Y.

ELISHA SMITH
Wayne County

SMITH, Elisha, private.
Placed on Pension Roll, Sept. 18, 1820, at the age of 70 yrs.
Service:—Massachusetts continental line.
Pension began May 2, 1818.
Annual allowance $96.00.   Sums received $1,425.32.
Inscribed under Act of Congress passed Mar. 18, 1818.
Remarks:—Transferred from Seneca Co., N. Y.

MARTIN SMITH
Monroe County

SMITH, Martin, private and corporal.
Placed on Pension Roll, Mar. 18, 1830.
Service:—25th U. S. infantry.
Pension began (1st) June 25, 1817; (2nd) Mar. 8, 1830.
Annual allowance (1st) $72.00; (2nd) $48.00.   Sums received (1st) $915.12; (2nd) $167.60.
Inscr.'bed under Act of Mar. 2, 1833; increased under Acts of military establishment.
Remarks:— This pensioner was allowed $6.00 per month, from June 25, 1817, until Mar. 11, 1830, as arrears of pension. See Act, Mar. 2, 1833.

REUBEN SMITH
St. Clair County

SMITH, Reuben, private.
Placed on Pension Roll, Apr. 20, 1833, at˜ age of 79 yrs.
Service:—Connecticut continental line.
Pension began Mar. 4, 1831.

Annual allowance $80.00. Sums received $240.00.
Inscribed under Act of Congress passed June 7, 1832.
Remarks:—Transferred from Cayuga Co., N. Y.
Ed. note:—In 1826, Reuben Smith was owner of
   Schr. "Packet" of 34 tons. *Mich. Hist. Colls.*,
   XXI, 364.

SILAS SPRAGUE
Oakland County

SPRAGUE, Silas, private.
Placed on Pension Roll, June 13, 1820.
Service:—Massachusetts continental line.
Pension began Mar. 1, 1820.
Annual allowance $96.00. Sums received $1,296.80.
Inscribed under Act of Congress passed Mar. 18, 1818.
Remarks:—Transferred from Broome Co., N. Y.
Ed. note:—About 1822, Silas Sprague located in Oak-
   land Co. *Mich. Hist. Colls.*, III, 569.

ELISHA STANLEY
St. Joseph County

STANLEY, Elisha, private.
Placed on Pension Roll, July 3, 1833, at age of 74 years.
Service:—Connecticut continental line.
Pension began Mar. 4, 1831.
Annual allowance $50.00. Sums received $150.00.
Inscribed under Act of Congress passed June 7, 1832.

DANIEL STEVENS
Wayne County

STEVENS, Daniel, private.
Placed on Pension Roll, Dec. 9, 1819.

Service:—U. S. artillery.

Pension began (1st) May 23, 1818; (2nd) Dec. 20, 1823; (3rd) Oct. 25, 1819.

Annual allowance (1st) $48.00; (2nd) $72.00; (3rd) $96.00. Sums received (1st) $267.73; (2nd) $421.00; (3rd) $274.66.

Inscribed and increased under Acts of military establishment.

HENRY STEVENS
Oakland County

STEVENS, Henry, private.

Placed on Pension Roll, July 12, 1820.

Service:—New York militia.

Pension began July 5, 1819.

Annual allowance $64.00.   Sums received $874.66.

Inscribed under Act passed Apr. 24, 1816.

Remarks:—Transferred from New York.

Ed. note:—"In 1834 Henry Stevens and Samuel Riblet made first settlement in township.   Henry Stevens on section thirteen, three miles east of Litchfield village, Hillsdale county. It was through the efforts of Henry Stevens that the town was named Litchfield." *Mich. Hist. Colls.*, I, 180.

JEREMIAH STONE
Wayne County

STONE, Jeremiah, private.

Placed on Pension Roll, Apr. 14, 1818, at the age of 76 yrs.

Service:—New Jersey continental line.

Pension began Apr. 1, 1818.

Annual allowance $96.00.   Sums received $1,488.80.
Inscribed under Act of Congress passed Mar. 18, 1818.
Ed. note:—Transferred from Saratoga Co., N. Y.
 "Name on Muster Roll of continental troops."
 Jerseymen in Revolution, p. 292.

SAMUEL STONE
Monroe County

STONE, Samuel, private.
Placed on Pension Roll, Sept. 10, 1828.
Service:—3rd reg., Connecticut line.
Pension began Mar. 3, 1826.
Annual allowance $80.00.   Sums received $320.00.
Inscribed under Act of Congress passed May 15, 1828.
Remarks:—Transferred from Onondaga Co., N. Y.

WARREN STONE
Wayne County

STONE, Warren, private.
Placed on Pension Roll, July 12, 1820.
Service:—New York Militia.
Pension began (1st) Nov. 9, 1814; (2nd) Mar. 22, 1832.
Annual allowance (1st) $48.00; (2nd) $72.00.   Sums
 received (1st) $833.72 (2nd) $104.54.
Inscribed under Acts of military establishment.
Remarks:—Transferred from New York.
Ed. note:—Name occurs on first tax roll of Plymouth,
 Wayne Co., Oct. 2, 1827; –Lot 13, T 1 S; 320 acres.

Real estate	$418.00
Personal	50.00
Total	$468.00
Tax	2.46

JONATHAN STRATTON
Wayne County

STRATTON, Jonathan, private.
Placed on Pension Roll, Oct. 5, 1819, at the age of 60 yrs.
Died Aug. 18, 1823.
Service:—Massachusetts continental line.
Pension began Apr. 24, 1818.
Annual allowance $96.00. Sums received $703.72.
Inscribed under Act of Congress passed Mar. 18, 1818.
Remarks:—Transferred from Erie Co., Pennsylvania.

HENRY SUTTON
Oakland County

SUTTON, Henry, private.
Placed on Pension Roll, May 9, 1822.
Service:—New York volunteers.
Pension began Feb. 4, 1822.
Annual allowance $72.00. Sums received $834.00.
Inscribed under Act of Apr. 24, 1816.
Remarks:—Transferred from New York.

CALEB TAFT
Macomb County

TAFT, Caleb, private.
Placed on Pension Roll, July 23, 1834, at the age of 82 yrs.
Service:—Massachusetts militia.
Pension began Mar. 4, 1831.
Annual allowance $20.00.
Inscribed under Act of Congress passed June 7, 1832.

JOHN TERHUNE
Washtenaw County

TERHUNE, John, ensign.
Placed on Pension Roll, Aug. 9, 1833, at age of 76 yrs.
Service:—New Jersey continental line.
Pension began Mar. 4, 1831.
Annual allowance $240.00.   Sums received $72.00.
Inscribed under Act of Congress passed June 7, 1832.
Ed. note:—See also Revolutionary Soldiers Buried in
   Mich.

WILLIAM N. TERRY
Oakland County

TERRY, William N., private.
Placed on Pension Roll, Aug. 9, 1833, at the age of
   74 yrs.
Service:—Pennsylvania continental line.
Pension began Mar. 4, 1831.
Annual allowance $80.00.   Sums received $240.00.
Inscribed under Act of Congress passed June 7, 1832.

AARON THOMAS
Wayne County

THOMAS, Aaron, private.
Placed on Pension Roll, Sept. 7, 1819, at the age of 72
   yrs.
Service:—Connecticut continental line.
Pension began Mar. 23, 1819.
Annual allowance $96.00.   Sums received $638.12.
Inscribed under Act of Congress passed Mar. 18, 1818.
Ed. note:—Name on highway tax of 1812; voted for
   Col. James M. Closkey, 1821; name on census roll of
   Detroit, 1827; *Mich. Hist. Colls.*

JONATHAN THOMPSON
Wayne County

THOMPSON, Jonathan, private.
Placed on Pension Roll, Aug. 2, 1822.
Service:—3rd U. S. infantry.
Pension began May 28, 1822.
Annual allowance $48.00.   Sums received $36.02.
Inscribed under Acts of military establishment.

JOSEPH TODD
Oakland County

TODD, Joseph, private.
Placed on Pension Roll, July 23, 1834, at the age of
     69 yrs.
Service:—New York militia.
Pension began Mar. 4, 1831.
Annual allowance $35.55.
Inscribed under Act of Congress passed June 7, 1832.
Ed. note:—The name of Joseph Todd occurs on the
     register of the 4th regiment, Orange Co., militia, N.
     Y. under Col. William Allison. *N. Y. in Revolu-
     tion*, p. 151.   Joseph Todd, Jr., among the "Land
     Bounty" men of 4th regiment, Orange Co., militia.
     N. Y. in Revolution, p. 251.   A Joseph Todd was
     born in Pa., Mar. 5, 1794; removed to Palmyra, N.
     Y.; a soldier in war of 1812; was in battle of Fort
     Erie.   Came to Mich. in 1819, crossing Lake Erie on
     second trip of "Walk-in-the-Water."   Died May
     15, 1882.   Married Polly Smith 1825, who died
     in 1868.   *Mich. Hist. Colls.*

JOHN M. VAN ALSTINE
Wayne County

VAN ALSTINE, John M., private.
Placed on Pension Roll, Apr. 7, 1832.
Service:—5th U. S. infantry.
Pension began Feb. 22, 1832.
Annual allowance $96.00.   Sums received $146.66.
Inscribed under Acts of military establishment.

JOSEPH VAN ATTER
Wayne County

VAN ATTER, Joseph, private.
Placed on Pension Roll, May 22, 1822, at the age of
70 yrs.
Service:—New York continental line.
Pension began Mar. 5, 1821.
Annual allowance $96.00.   Sums received $1,200.00.
Inscribed under Act of Congress passed Mar. 18, 1818.

SAMUEL WALDRON
Washtenaw County

WALDRON, Samuel, ensign.
Placed on Pension Roll, July 1, 1834, at the age of 73
yrs.
Service:—New Jersey continental line.
Pension began Mar. 4, 1831.
Annual allowance $80.00.
Inscribed under Act of Congress passed June 7, 1832.

JOHN WALKER
Macomb County

WALKER, John, private.
Placed on Pension Roll, Dec. 31, 1822.
Died Dec. 31, 1825.
Service:—Michigan cavalry.
Pension began Nov. 25, 1822.
Annual allowance $96.00.   Sums received $489.60.
Inscribed under Act of Apr. 24, 1816.

JOHN WALTERS
Wayne County

WALTERS, John, private.
Placed on Pension Roll, May 21, 1833, at the age of
74 yrs.
Service:—New Jersey militia.
Pension began Mar. 4, 1831.
Annual allowance $56.66.   Sums received $169.98.
Inscribed under Act of Congress passed June 7, 1832.
Remarks:—Transferred from New York.
Ed. note:—Name on official "Roster of Continental
troops." *Jerseymen in Revolution*, p. 306. "3rd.
battalion, 1st establishment Capt. Flanagan's Co.;
3rd battalion, 2nd est., 3rd regiment."

ABEL WARREN
Macomb County

WARREN, Abel, sergeant.
Placed on Pension Roll, July 28, 1818.
Service:—23rd U. S. infantry.

Pension began (1st) Dec. 1, 1813; (2nd) Feb. 4, 1835.
Annual allowance_ $48.00; $96.00. Sums received
$948.40.
Inscribed under Acts of military establishment.
Remarks:—Transferred from New York.
Ed. note:—Rev. Abel Warren—born in Washington
Co., N. Y., 1789, served in War of 1812, severely
wounded and taken prisoner at Queenstown Heights,
paroled and sent home. Married Sarah Hooker, of
Vt. Moved to Mich., 1820, buying eighty acres near
Pontiac, July 2, 1824. Moved to W. ½ of S. W. ¼
S. 4 in Shelby Twp., Macomb Co., where he lived
until his death in 1862. This "Soldier of the Cross"
was the first man licensed to preach in Territory of
Michigan. See *Mich. Hist. Colls.*, Vol. 18.

THOMAS WATTS
Oakland County

WATTS, Thomas, private.
Placed on Pension Roll, May 11, 1820.
Service:—New York militia.
Pension began May 11, 1820.
Annual allowance $48.00. Sums received $639.20.
Inscribed under Act of Apr. 24, 1816.
Remarks:—Transferred from N. Y.
Ed. note:—"Among those who located land in 1823, in
what is now (1874) known as Moscow was, Thomas
Watts." See Hillsdale Co., 1829–1836 by F. M.
Holloway in *Mich. Hist. Colls.*, I, 172. Oct. 8,
1825 land entry:—Section 26, 27, Oakland Co.
Mich. Hist. Colls., II, 449. *N. Y. in the Revolution*,
pp. 96, 124, gives this name among the soldiers whose
service had not been identified; again with the names
of the 13th regiment, Albany Co. militia, under
Col. John McCrea.

ROSWELL WEBSTER
Macomb County

WEBSTER, Roswell, private.
Placed on Pension Roll, Sept. 17, 1820.
Service:—(1st) New Jersey militia; (2nd) Revolutionary war.
Pension began (1st) Feb. 19, 1820; (2nd) Dec. 18, 1828.
Annual allowance (1st) $48.00; (2nd) $96.00.   Sums received (1st) $423.60; (2nd) $460.48.
Inscribed under Acts passed Apr., 1812; increased Mar., 1819.
Remarks:—Transferred from N. Y., Mar. 4, 1826.
Ed. note:—In 1826, land, in section one Macomb Co., entered in the name of Roswell Webster. "He was active in formation of the first district school of Macomb Co., in 1828." *Mich. Hist. Colls.* A private on the muster roll of *Officers and Men of New Jersey in the Revolution*, p. 814.

THOMAS WHIPPLE
Lenawee County

WHIPPLE, Thomas, private.
Placed on Pension Roll, May 3, 1819, at the age of 80 yrs.
Service:—New Hampshire continental line.
Pension began Apr. 21, 1818.
Annual allowance $96.00.   Sums received $1,425.32.
Inscribed under Act of Congress passed Mar. 18, 1818.
Remarks:—Transferred from Albany Co.

DE LAFAYETTE WILCOX
"Chicago County"

WILCOX, De LaFayette, 2nd lieutenant.
Placed on Pension Roll, June 18, 1828.

Service:—25th U. S. infantry.
Pension began June 18, 1828.
Annual allowance $180.00.   Sums received $463.20.
Inscribed under Acts of military establishment.
Ed. note:—De LaFayette Wilcox, Connecticut army.
Private and sergeant in 25th infantry, May, 1812 to
Nov., 1813; ensign 25th infantry, 16th Nov., 1813;
2nd lieut., 14th Mar., 1814; 1st lieut., 2nd Oct.,
1814; transferred to 6th infantry 17th May, 1815;
transferred to 5th infantry, 1st June, 1821; capt.
1st Apr., 1822; brevet major 1st Apr., 1832 "for
ten years faithful service in one grade"; died 3rd
Jan., 1842. *Hist. Register of U. S. Army.* "Capt.
Wilcox of the garrison at Fort Brady in 1828".
"Commander of the Post at Sault Ste. Marie was one
of the elders of the Presbyterian church at its organization; was succeeded in 1832 by Major John Fowle".
"Major Fowle later became Professor of military
tactics at West Point and Major De LaFayette Wilcox became commandant at Fort Dearborn, at
Chicago." *Mich. Hist. Colls.*

JAMES WITHERELL
Wayne County

WITHERELL, James, ensign.
Placed on Pension Roll, Aug. 27, 1831.
Service:—11th reg. Massachusetts continental line.
Pension began Mar. 3, 1826.
Annual allowance $240.00.   Sums received $2,160.00.
Inscribed under Act of Congress passed May 15, 1828.
Remarks:—N. S. Sprague, Hon. R. C. Mallory and
Hon. Lewis Cass, agents.   See also Revolutionary
Soldiers Buried in Michigan.

LEONARD WITTING
Oakland County

WITTING, Leonard, corporal.
Placed on Pension Roll, June 18, 1818.
Service:—19th U. S. infantry.
Pension began Oct. 19, 1814.
Annual allowance $96.00.   Sums received $586.C£.
Inscribed under Acts of military establishment.

HAROLD A. FURLONG, M. H.,
Lieutenant, 353rd Infantry, 89th Division.

MICHIGAN "MEDAL OF HONOR" MEN

Soldiers of Michigan who have been decorated with the highest award, the Medal of Honor conferred by Congress for most distinguished gallantry in action or other soldier-like qualities, 1814–1918.

CHAPTER III

MICHIGAN "MEDAL OF HONOR" MEN

The pages of history and literature are crowded with the deeds of heroes, of chivalry honored by its king, with national periods which have incited brave deeds as the common duty of all men, and evolved the greater hero who in hazardous enterprise should distinguish himself above his fellows. Greece, Rome, Italy, France, England, through art and literature have idealized their most distinguished heroes, each age adding its deeds and characteristics to a composite picture, until each nation has produced its great traditional hero whose deeds are living forces in the world,—national standards of heroism which raise or lower the world standard.

America, secure in its youth and strength, has indifferently filed away in government archives the records of its own most heroic men,—a great poetic treasure store, awaiting the inspired minstrel whose clearer vision may "follow the gleam," who may immortalize in worthy epic the deeds of our own "Legion of Honor," sing in worthy meter the valor of our Michigan men,— their deeds and place in history which the world of art has epitomized on the surface of coins; heroes who have received the nation's highest award, the MEDAL OF HONOR, conferred by special Act of Congress for most conspicuous gallantry in action.

The modern medal, invented during the Italian renaissance, has been used by Italy, France, England, and Germany, not only to commemorate national events,

but for individual award to incite bravery in troops
or encourage great enterprise. Our forefathers, con-
cerned for the safety of our struggling nation, feared
the medal's power in the hands of intriguing rulers,
and so prohibited its acceptance from any foreign
state, and frugal in its own usage, reserved the Congressional MEDAL OF HONOR as the highest form of
award.

We find a record of but forty-nine Congressional
Medals issued before the Civil War; but on that "honor
roll" from General George Washington, for the capture
of Boston in 1776, to Dr. Frederick H. Rose of the
British navy, "for humanity," we note the challenged
democracy and glimpse an American standard of
bravery for soldier and sailor, citizen and alien.

July 12, 1862, a joint resolution authorized the pre-
sentation of a medal of honor by Congress to such non-
commissioned officers and privates as should most
distinguish themselves by gallantry in action and other
soldier-like qualities; the subsequent enactment of
March 3, 1863, amended the Act to include officers.
An order issued in 1897, under Sec'y of War Russell
A. Alger states: "In order that the Congressional
Medal of Honor may be deserved, service must have
been performed in action, of such conspicuous character
as to clearly distinguish the man for gallantry and
intrepidity above his comrades, service that involved
extreme jeopardy of life, or the performance of extra-
ordinarily hazardous duty. Recommendations for decoration will be judged by this standard of extraordinary merit, and incontestable proof of performance of
service will be exacted."

Out of the millions who have served in the armies
of the United States, about three thousand men have

received the Congressional Medal of Honor; of these only four have received two medals, and two of the four were Michigan men.

In this pageant of the "Legion of Honor" whom may we claim as Michigan men, those in service under the Michigan colors or the adopted son and the native-born? Which are the Michigan men?

If by Michigan men we include the resident or the native-born serving in army organizations outside the State, we have an incomplete list extending from Maj. Gen. Alexander Macomb (born in Detroit), Commander-in-chief of the American forces in 1814, awarded a commemorative medal of honor for the victory of Plattsburg—to the eight medallists of Michigan's company B, in the 47th Ohio, who, with steam tug and two barges of food attempted to run the enemy's batteries at Vicksburg, Miss. May 3, 1863; namely, Capt. W. H. Ward, Corp'l's Henry Lewis and Nash, private Ballen, and Hack, Hodges, Sype and Peters; Corp'l Lewis and Private Peters receiving their award for this deed of 1863 on the 17th of April, 1917.

If by Michigan men we refer to the adopted son or the native-born enlisted under the Michigan colors marching steadily beside the "Starry 'Old Glory' waging its wars for humanity's sake"—then in the din of battle we find them, and valiant the deeds, and gallant the men, whom Michigan may claim.

First, the two with the double accolade: one a hero of old St. Joseph County whose first medal was awarded when as an officer in the 19th infantry, ahead of his own men he led a counter charge under a galling fire, singly entering the enemy's line, capturing and bringing back two commissioned officers, fully armed, besides a stand of Georgia's colors—Frank Dwight Baldwin, captain of co. D., 19th Mich. inf., who again in 1874 when lieutenant of the 5th U. S. infantry, on the plains of Texas he rescued, with two companies, two white girls, by a voluntary attack upon Indians whose superior numbers and strong position would have warranted delay for reinforcements, but which delay would have permitted the killing of the two captive girls and the escape of the Indians,— fearless in the duties of an officer, fearless in his protection of helpless women, a Michigan warrior measuring fully up to the national standard of heroism.

To appreciate the next winner of two medals we need as background the 6th Mich. cavalry to whom on April 9, 1865, Gen. George Custer said: "During the past six months, though in most instances confronted by superior numbers, you have captured from the enemy, in open battle, 111 pieces of field artillery, 65 battle flags and upwards of 10,000 prisoners of war, including seven general officers. . . . . You have never lost a gun, never lost a color, never been defeated; and notwithstanding the numerous engagements in which you have borne a prominent part, you have captured every piece of artillery which the enemy has opened upon you." With such a background, clearly distinguished in daring stands, Thomas W. Custer, second lieut., co. B, 6th Mich. cavalry, twice awarded a medal of honor by Congress, for gallant daring in capturing battle flags. History records that in their famous cavalry charges he often rode neck and neck with his more famous brother; that when he captured his second flag at Sailor's Creek (April 6, 1865) he leaped his horse over the enemy's works and captured two stands of colors, having his horse killed under him as the enemy standard-bearer shot Custer in the face. It is further said of him that day that though so severely wounded, he secured another mount and with undiminished enthusiasm was preparing to charge again when his brother stopped him and requested him to go to the rear. As he paid no attention to the request, General Custer placed him under arrest and sent him to the rear.

In this review on the field of honor the old "Stonewall" brigade, Michigan's 17th infantry, should hold first rank for the number of Congressional medals of honor won. Organized in Detroit under command of Col. William H. Withington, of Jackson, it engaged the enemy two weeks after it was mustered in; and as it waged its war for unity in freedom, many of its men were breveted in rank and nine awarded the Congressional (army) medal of honor. They were, General Withington, then captain of co. B, who was awarded a medal for remaining on the battle field of Bull Run under heavy fire to succor a wounded officer; Frederick Alber, pvt., co. A, rescued a lieutenant of his regiment who had been captured by three of the enemy,—Alber shot one and took the other two prisoners to the Union lines; Falconer, corp'l., co. A, Shepard, corp'l., co. E, and Kelley, pvt., co. E., destroyed buildings, within the enemy's lines, which harbored enemy sharpshooters, disregarded an order to retire, remained under fire from the advancing enemy until the complete destruction of the buildings was assured; and McFall, serg., co. E., at Spottsylvania, May 12, 1864, "captured the colonel commanding the Confederate brigade that charged the Union batteries, and on the same day rescued an officer of his regiment from the enemy; the regimental color bearer, Joseph E. Brandle, having been twice wounded, shot through the eye, staggered blindly onward with his colors until ordered to the rear by his commander; Charles A. Thompson. serg., co. D, carried the State colors at Spottsylvania, Va., after the regiment was surrounded and all resistance seemed useless, fought on single-handed for the colors, and refused to give them up until he was ordered to do so by his own superior officers."

The ninth medallist on the Seventeenth's honor roll, Brig. Gen. Frederick W. Swift—then lieut. col.—"seized the colors, at Lenoir Station, Nov. 16, 1863, and rallied the regiment after three color bearers had been shot, and the regiment demoralized and in imminent danger of capture." Does not one's spirit stand "at attention" as Michigan's color bearers pass by,—with them the honorary escort who captured enemy colors from an equally valiant enemy:—Corp'l Plant, co. F., 14th Mich. inf. at Bentonville, N. C., Mar. 19, 1865; and Serg. Noll, co. D, 20th Mich. inf., May 12, 1864 at Spottsylvania, Va.; each rushed into the midst of the enemy and rescued the colors—the color-bearer falling, fatally wounded.—Clute, Fall, Cole, Fox, Custer, Crocker, Kemp, Mundell, Sancrainte, Holton, Norton, Savacool, Alonzo Smith, Menter, Youngs, McHale, each one worthy of the nation's highest award. Following them in close order are the men who would not retreat:—Captain Haistings, co. M, 5th Mich. cavalry, while in command of a squadron in the rear guard of a cavalry division, then retiring before the advance of the enemy infantry, having received orders to abandon guns and retire, repelled the attack and saved the guns; and Sidney Haight, corp'l., co. E, 1st Mich. S. S. at Petersburg, Va., instead of retreating, remained in the captured works, regardless of his personal safety, and exposed to the enemy's fire, boldly, deliberately returned it until the enemy was upon him. . . . . In describing the engagement at Petersburg in which the 1st Mich. S. S. and the 20th Mich. took active part, Lieut. Col. Byron M. Cutcheon commanding the 20th Mich. inf. writes: "About 1:30 P. M. I came back to our lines to obtain water and ammunition for the men; before I could return the last charge was made and nearly all our forces came back. It was some time before I learned that any part of my command was still in the rebel fort, but at three P. M. our colors were still flying on their works, defended by about thirty of my command. . .; of these about ten made their escape, the remainder were taken prisoners, among them, all that remained of the color guard, of whom only two remained uninjured. So far as I can learn, the colors of the Twentieth and the Second Mich. were the last displayed on the rebel fort. Charles H. DePuy of the 1st Mich. S. S. was awarded a Medal of Honor; as an old artillerist he aided Gen. Bartlett in working the discarded guns of the dismantled fort, keeping the enemy at bay as long as ammunition lasted." Maj. Cutcheon was also a medallist, for distinguished gallantry in leading his regiment in a charge on a house occupied by the enemy.

Another type of bravery is pictured in the guerilla warfare: Private James H. Robinson, co. B, 3rd Mich. cavalry as he successfully defended himself, single-handed, against seven guerillas, killing the leader and driving off the remainder; and Andrew Traynor, corp'l., co. D, 1st Mich. cavalry, who having been surprised and captured by a detachment of guerillas siezed the arms of the guard, killed two and enabled all of their prisoners to escape. Our sister State, Wisconsin, with whom our military history is so closely allied, has a medallist who not only defeated seven guerillas, but took them captive and brought them into camp. These deeds form plots for stories rivaling in interest Robin Hood and Little John, Friar Tuck and all the outlaws of Sherwood Forest, who were perhaps fortunate to have lived before American efficiency could actuate the Sheriff of Nottingham in suppressing lawless warfare.

Quite as thrilling as the deeds of guerilla fighters are those of the messengers:—Sergeant Cornelius M. Hadley, co. F, 9th Mich. cavalry, who, at Knoxville, Tenn., Nov. 20, 1863, "with one companion, voluntarily carried through the enemy's lines important dispatches from General Grant to General Burnsides, then besieged within Knoxville, and brought back replies, his comrade's horse being killed and the man taken prisoner;" and Sergt. Joseph S. Keen, co. D, 13th Mich. infantry, "while an escaped prisoner of war, within the enemy's lines, witnessed an important movement of the enemy, made his way through the lines and brought news of the movement to Sherman's army." Though we may not tell in detail the story of each medallist, the list would be incomplete in interest without Sancrainte, co. B, 15th Mich. inf., scaling the enemy's breastworks, signalling to his commander to charge, and in single combat capturing the enemy's colors. Major General Loyd Wheaton, born in Pennfield, Mich. as lieut. col. in the 8th Illinois infantry at Fort Blakely, Apr. 9, 1865, led the right wing of his regiment, springing through an embrasure, the first to enter the enemy's works, against a strong fire of artillery and musketry. Nor can the story be omitted which is told by Col. William L. Stoughton concerning W. G. Whitney and the 11th Michigan at Chickamauga, Sept. 20, 1863: "Our troops without exception, maintained their ground with unfaltering courage and the few who recoiled from the storm of bullets were speedily rallied and returned with renewed ardor . . . The enemy was in heavy force and fought with the most determined obstinacy. As fast as their ranks were thinned by our fire, they were filled up again by fresh troops. They pressed forward and charged our lines, firing across our breastworks and planted their colors within 100 feet of our own . . . . Our ammunition became exhausted during the fight and every cartridge that could be found on the persons of the killed and wounded as well as in the boxes of the prisoners were taken and distributed to the men . . . William G. Whitney, serg't., co. B, 11th Michigan infantry, as the enemy was about to charge went outside the temporary Union works among the dead and wounded enemy and removed their cartridge boxes, bringing the same within the Union lines, the much needed ammunition being used to good effect in repulsing the enemy."

Then there are the records of Col. Orlando Willcox, 1st Mich. inf., who led repeated charges at Bull Run until taken prisoner; Capt. Edward Hill, co. K, 16th Mich. inf., leading the skirmish line up to the very muzzles of the enemy's guns; 1st Lieut. James I. Christiancy, co. D, 9th Mich. cavalry, while acting as aide led a part of the line and turned the tide of battle; Sergt. Patrick Irwin, co. H, 14th Mich. inf., in a charge against the entrenched enemy, demanded and received the surrender of a Confederate general officer and his command; Romeyn, the Indian fighter; French, Sidman,

Smith, Forman, Shafter,—names which stand for grim unflinching courage, men though wounded, fighting until fainting, refusing to go to the rear until carried there.

Were we painting a composite picture of Michigan's ideal hero we would gladly add the expression of mercy and self-sacrifice exemplified by Sergeant Tobin of co. C, 9th Michigan infantry, who returned in the face of the advancing enemy and rescued from impending death Major Stevens, thrown from his horse; Sergeant Luce, co. E, 4th Michigan infantry, acting as orderly, voluntarily carrying the wounded from the ground in front of the crater while exposed to heavy fire; Assistant Surgeon George E. Ranney, of the 2nd Michigan cavalry, going to the aid of the wounded lying under heavy fire between the two lines. The giant heart of our United States finds no greater avenue of expression than through the deeds of the physicians and surgeons trained in the every-day school of self-sacrifice and hazardous duty who repeatedly merit decorations for most extraordinary heroism as they extend mercy and help to friend and foe al·ke.

We are told that in the days of Richard Coeur de Lion, when a truce existed between the Christian armies of the third crusade and the infidel forces under Sultan Saladin, Sir Kenneth, on his way to Syria, encountered a Saracen emir whom he unhorsed, and that, "Thereafter they rode together . . . discoursing on love and necromancy." We also read that the Teuton, Conrad of Montserrat, desiring to be King of Jerusalem, incited Leopold of Austria to plant Austria's colors in the center of England's camp, and later, with characteristic Teutonic diplomacy, stole the colors of England's king. Not being permitted

to fight the Teuton himself, King Richard accepted the
services of the Saracen emir to find a knight to act
as substitue. "Great was the surprise of King Richard
when the Saracen appeared with a brilliant retinue and
proved to be not only the great physician who had
healed him of a fever, had saved Sir Kenneth's life, but
was none other than Saladin the infidel sultan."
Scenes shift, the ages pass and side by side with these
Old World heroes, chivalry has ranked our Michigan
men, side by side in the Old World trenches, of the
same fine spirit, staunch, loyal, protectors of the weak,
possessing the unconquerable determination which
wins, but wins with a spirit of chivalry. Michigan's
history lacks neither great heroes nor records of great
heroic deeds, but its "Legion of Honor" does need a
brilliant minded Merlin with a literary magic who may
mark in letters of gold each hero's place at the Round
Table of a State's remembrance.

FREDERICK ALBER, M. H.
17th Mich. Infantry

ALBER, FREDERICK, Manchester. Enlisted in co. A,
17th inf., July 2, 1862, at Manchester for 3 yrs.
Age 24.

Mustered Aug. 19, 1862. Mustered out at Delancy
House, D. C., June 3, 1865. Resided later in Elba,
Mich.

The 17th Mich. inf. was organized at Detroit, 1862,
sent to Washington, D. C., Aug. 27, 1862 under the
command of Col. Wm. H. Withington, Jackson;
Surgeon Abram R. Calkins, Allegan; Ass't Surgeons
Jonathan Beviere, Grand Rapids, and Albert Daniels,
Richland; Adj. Wm. V. Richards, Ann Arbor; Q. M.

Charles Ford, Jackson. Co. A.—Capt. Loren L. Comstock, Adrian; Lieut. John S. Vreeland, Adrian; 2nd Lt. Richard A. Watts, Adrian.

Sept. 14, engaged the enemy at South Mt. and "on the crest of the mountain drove the enemy from behind his stonewall defences and sent him retreating down the slope of the mountain" which secured for the 17th the title of the "Stonewall Regiment." Of the 500 men in this engagement 140 were killed or wounded two weeks from the time they were mustered in.

The 17th fought bravely through many engagements of the war until it crossed the Rapidan at Germanias Ford and on the sixth of May engaged in the desperate battle of the Wilderness and campaign following; on May 12 was practically annihilated.

Medal of Honor Award:—Private Alber was awarded the Medal of Honor, July 30, 1898. May 12, 1864, at Spottsylvania, Va., "Frederick Alber, a private in co. A, 17th Michigan infantry bravely rescued a lieutenant of his regiment, who had been captured by a party of Confederates, by shooting one, knocking over another with the butt of his musket, and taking them both prisoners."

FRANK DWIGHT BALDWIN, M. H.
Capt. company D, 19th Michigan Infantry

BALDWIN, FRANK DWIGHT, major-gen. U. S. A.
Born, Manchester, Michigan, June 26th, 1842.
Son of Francis Leonard and Betsey Ann (Richards) Baldwin.
Educated in Constantine, Mich., public schools; Hillsdale College. LL.D. conferred by Hillsdale College.
Married Alice Blackwood, of Northville, Mich., Jan. 10, 1867.

Military Service:—General Baldwin, one of the four
soldiers in the United States, who have been twice
awarded the Medal of Honor, has the following
record of service:—
Entered service from Constantine in Chandler Horse
Guards as second lieutenant at organization, Aug.
18, 1861, at White Pigeon, for three years.
Age 19.
Mustered, Sept. 19, 1861; mustered out at Coldwater,
Nov. 22, 1861.
Re-entered service in company D, 19th infantry at
organization as first lieutenant, July 21, 1862, at
Constantine for three years.
Commissioned, July 28. Mustered, Sept. 5, 1862.
Commissioned captain, Jan. 23, 1864. Mustered, Feb.
11, 1864.
Commissioned lieut. colonel, June 15, 1865.
Mustered out near Washington, D. C., June 10, 1865.
Second lieutenant and first lieutenant, Nineteenth
U. S. inf., Feb. 23, 1866.
Transferred to Thirty-seventh infantry, Sept. 21, 1866.
Transferred to Fifth infantry, May 19, 1869.
Captain, March 20, 1879.
Major, April 26, 1898.
Lieutenant colonel and inspector general, volunteers,
May 9, 1898.
Discharged from volunteer service, May 12, 1899.
Transferred from Fifth to Third U. S. infantry, Nov.
3, 1899.
Lieutenant colonel Fourth infantry, Dec. 18, 1899.
Transferred to First infantry, July 23, 1901.
Colonel Twenty-seventh infantry, July 26, 1901.
Brigadier general, June 9, 1902.

Brevet captain, U. S. A., Feb. 27, 1890: for gallant service against Indians on the Salt Fork of the Red River, Texas, Aug. 30, 1874; and on McClellan's Creek, Texas, Nov., 1874.

Major for gallant and successful attack on Sitting Bull's camp of Indians on Red Water River, Montana, Dec. 18, 1876; and conspicuous gallantry in action against Indians at Wolf Mountain, Montana, Jan. 8, 1877.

"Commanded first body of civilized troops that ever successfully reached the south shore of Lake Lanao (Island of Mindanao) and after desperate fighting with Moros at battle of Bylan, May 2, 1902, completely overcame them; the Moros losing over 300 out of 330."

In command of S. W. Division.

Retired, June 20, 1906.

Nominated major-general, Dec. 10, 1915.

Adjutant general of Colorado, 1916–19.

Medal of Honor award:—Frank D. Baldwin, captain co. D, 19th Mich. inf., on Dec. 31, 1891 was awarded a Medal of Honor for conspicuous bravery at Peach Tree Creek, July 20, 1864, when he led his company in a countercharge under a galling fire ahead of his own men and singly entered the enemy's line bringing back two commissioned officers, fully armed, besides a guidon of a Georgia regiment.

2nd Medal of Honor award:—Baldwin, Frank D., 1st lieutenant 5th U. S. infantry, was awarded a Medal of Honor on Nov. 28, 1894 for bravery at McClellan's Creek, Texas, Nov. 8, 1874. Rescued with two companies two white girls, by a voluntary attack upon Indians whose superior numbers and strong position would have warranted delay for reinforcements, but which delay would have permitted the Indians to escape and kill their captives.

"Hdqt. 19th Mich.

Near Atlanta, Ga., July 27, 1864.

. . . On the morning of the 20th we moved after the enemy a short distance in the direction of Atlanta. Crossing Peach Tree Creek, the regiment 300 strong was formed in the rear of the Eighty-fifth Indiana. While in this position the enemy was discovered to be advancing in heavy force, but the brigade being promptly advanced met the enemy a short distance in the rear of the position which had been occupied by our pickets, when a severe engagement ensued. The fight raged furiously in this position for the space of ten or fifteen minutes, when the Nineteenth was ordered up to the support of the front line. Moving promptly up, a few well directed volleys from the whole line compelled the rebels to fall back. Seeing the advantage, the regiment, with those with whom they were fighting side by side, advanced at a double quick until they reached the crest of the ridge. In this position they remained for four hours, assisting as best they could in suppressing any rebel demonstration made in their front. At nine p. m. the regiment was relieved by the 33rd Indiana and moving to the rear, camped for the night". From the report by D. Anderson, captain commanding regiment.

The Nineteenth was organized at Dowagiac under the direction of Col. Henry C. Gilbert of Coldwater, and was composed of companies recruited in the 2nd Congressional District.

The regiment was mustered into service, Sept. 5th, 1862.

The field, staff and line officers at organization were as follows:

Colonel Henry C. Gilbert, Coldwater; Lieut. Col. David Bacon, Niles; Major William R. Shafter, Gales-

burg; Surgeon Wm. E. Clark, Dowagiac; Assistant
Surg. John Benett, Centerville; 2nd Assistant Surg.
Leander D. Tompkins, Cassopolis; Adj. Hamlet B.
Adams, Coldwater; Quartermaster Warren Chapman,
St. Joseph; Chaplin Israel Cogshall, Coldwater.

Company D:—Captain Hazen W Brown, Constantine; 1st Lt. Frank D. Baldwin, Constantine; 2nd Lt.
Charles W. Funda, Centerville.

"The Nineteenth left its camp, Sept. 14, for Cincinnati, O., and became a part of the first division,
Army of Kentucky, which afterward formed part of the
Army of the Cumberland.   Its first serious engagement
was at Thompson's Station, Tenn., March 5th, 1863
where it proved its characteristic qualities of heroism
which afterwards character zed it in many a hard
fought field.

"The Confederates made three separate charges upon
the brigade which were gallantly repulsed, in one of
which the Nineteenth captured the colors of a Mississippi regiment. The engagement lasted five hours until
the ammunition was exhausted and the overwhelming
numbers compelled it to surrender.—But not until
the enemy paid dearly for the victory."

After the exchange of officers and the enlisted men
paroled the regiment was reorganized at Camp Chase
and in June, returned to Nashville.

"They were also at Resaca, May 15, 1864; Cassville,
New Hope Church, Golgotha, Culps Farm, Peach Tree
Creek, siege of Atlanta, Savannah, Ga., Averysboro, N.
C., Bentonville, N. C. and in many other engagements.

"The Nineteenth was a part of the 2nd brigade, 3rd
division, 20 corps when Sherman started on his march
to the sea."

Record of Service of Michigan Volunteers.

Ed. note:—At a banquet given in honor of General
John Pershing, in Denver, Colorado, January 20,
1920, General Pershing paid the following friendly
tribute to General Baldwin: "One thing has added
greatly to my pleasure and that is to meet again my
old time and distinguished friend, Frank D. Baldwin,
I had the pleasure of serving under General Baldwin,
and took my apprenticeship in the Philippines
under him and tonight I acknowledge that what-
ever military training I may have is due largely to
General Baldwin's bringing up." Though now (1920)
the adjutant general of Colorado, Michigan claims
this national hero, who has served through five
wars, because he was born, educated and married
in Michigan and began his military career in the old
Michigan Horse Guards.

FREDERICK BALLEN, M. H.
47th Ohio Infantry

BALLEN, FREDERICK.   Enlisted in co. B, 47th Ohio inf.,
June 15, 1861, at Adrian, for three years.
Age 27.
Mustered, July 29, 1861.
Mustered out at Columbus, O., Aug. 31, 1864.
Medal of Honor award:—Frederick Ballen, pvt., co. B,
47th Ohio inf., was issued a Medal of Honor, on the
6th of Nov., 1908, for heroic action May 3, 1863, at
Vicksburg, Miss.   Was one of a party that volun-
teered and attempted to run the enemy's batteries
with a steam tug and two barges loaded with sub-
sistence stores.
Other names cited for the same action are:
John Hack, pvt. co. B, 47th Ohio inf. (Issued Feb.
5, 1907). Addison J. Hodges, co. B, 47th Ohio inf.

(Issued Dec. 31, 1907).   Henry Lewis, corp. co. B, 47th Ohio inf.   (Issued April 17, 1917).   Henry C. Peters, pvt. co. B, 47th Ohio inf.   (Issued April 17, 1917).

Forty-seventh Ohio Infantry.

In June, 1861, a company of infantry was organized by William H. Ward of Adrian.   There being no vacancy for this company in Michigan, its services were offered to the Governor of Ohio, accepted by him, and assigned to the 47th Ohio infantry as co. B.   It was mustered into the U. S. service at Camp Denison, Ohio, July 29, 1861; and mustered out at Little Rock, Ark., Aug. 11, 1865.   It saw service in West Va., Miss. and Georgia and took part in the last engagements between Generals Sherman and Johnston at Bentonville, N. C., March 19 and 21, 1865.

JOSEPH E. BRANDLE, M. H.
17th Mich. Infantry

BRANDLE, JOSEPH E., enlisted in co. G, 17th Mich. infantry, April 24, 1861, at Burr Oak, for three months.

Age 22.

Mustered, May 1, 1861.   Mustered out at Detroit, Aug. 7, 1861.

Re-entered service as color bearer.

Enlisted in co. C, 17th infantry, July 1, 1861, at Colon, for three years.   Mustered, Aug 18, 1862.   Wounded in action near Knoxville, Tenn., Nov. 16, 1863.   Discharged near Petersburg, Va., on account of wounds received Sept. 24, 1864.   Loss of eye.

Later residence Coldwater, Mich.

Medal of Honor award:—Issued to Joseph E. Brandle by the War Department, July 20, 1897.

Ground of award: "Nov. 16, 1863, at Lenoir, Tenn.
while color bearer of his regiment, having been twice
wounded and the sight of cne eye destroyed still
held to the colors until ordered to the rear by his
commander."
Report of Lieut. Col. Lorin L. Comstock, 17th Mich.
inf.
Hdqts. 17th Regiment, Mich. inf.
       Knoxville, Tenn., Nov. 21, 1863.
   Lieutenant:—In compliance with orders I have the
honor to make the following report of my command
from the 14th to the 17th of this month:—
   On the morning of the 14th instant, we received
orders at 7 o'clock to pack all baggage and be ready
to move at a moment's notice, leaving nothing behind.
At 12 M. the assembly sounded and we moved off
towards Loudon, following the 2nd. Mich. till near 7
or 8 p. m. and halted in woods rest.ng in line of battle in
front of the enemy.
   Between 3 and 4 o'clock the next morning the 15th,
we marched quietly to left front towards Lenoir, where
we arrived near 12 M.   Here we stacked arms and the
men made coffee.   Moved again between 3 and 4 p. m.
and took position with the brigade back of the village
on the Kingston road threw out skirmishers and lay
in line of battle till daylight when we fell back to the
railroad stacked arms and rested while the troops
passed to the rear.   Here we received notice that our
regiment was to form the rear guard and cover the
retreat towards Knoxville.   Three companies under
Captain Tyler and Phillips and Lieut. Billingsley were
thrown out as skirmishers under the general super-
vision of Capt. F. W. Swift (acting major).
   We were overtaken and attacked by the enemy at

9:30 a. m. at ———— Creek near Campbell's Station. Col. W. Humphrey commanding the brigade sent me orders to hold the enemy at all hazards until the brigade could find a better position and form line. The enemy crowded upon us in overwhelming numbers, and here was the most trying part of the day. The men fought well and held their ground until flanked upon left and right. We then fell back in line of battle upon the open field in front of the brigade where Col. Humphrey ordered us to the rear. We had marched but a few rods when we received orders to form on the left of the 20th Michigan and extend skirmishers farther to the left to prevent being flanked The enemy pressed boldly forward and the whole brigade was soon hotly engaged. Still they crowded us but we fought them determinedly. They were flanking us on both right and left, our skirmishers were falling back in much confusion before their strong lines and everything looked gloomy; but Col. Humphrey came to us just in time, and ordered me to charge and drive the enemy back out of the woods. The men sprang forward with cheer after cheer, and the 20th coming gallantly to our aid, we drove them back out of the woods and over the field in double quick. Col. Humphrey at once ordered us to march in retreat and under cover of the shock given by the charge we marched slowly and in good order to the large brick house in the open field. Here we filed in by flank and crossed the road. The enemy came down upon us from the woods and high weeds in front. Col. Humphrey commanded "Fire by file" and after one round he ordered us to the right of the brigade. Here we lay in line until the brigade was relieved by the Colonel commanding 2nd brigade when we fell back to the creek, stacked arms and rested until 3:30 p. m. when we marched back to the rear of the batteries, stacked arms and rested till dark. We then fell in and marched toward Knoxville reaching it on the morning of the 17th near 4 o'clock.

I cannot speak in too high terms of all the officers and men of my regiment but will mention some who are especially deserving of notice. I am greatly indebted to Capt. F. W. Swift (acting major), Capt. John Tyler and Adj. R. A. Watts for their brave, gallant and efficient conduct during the entire day. The Captain after being severely wounded used every effort to inspire steadiness among the men until faint and exhausted he was borne from the field. Among the bravest of the men were Color Sergeant Joseph E. Brandle who being wounded severely, a ball entering his head passing through the right eye, still held to the colors until ordered to the rear by myself; and Charles Thompson, carrier of the State colors, was equally gallant, and called upon the men to stand firmly by the standard he bore; also Corp'l A. P. Curtis, who took the colors from the sergeant and bore them gallantly through the remainder of the day.

Yours respectfully,

L. L. Comstock,

Lieut.-Col. Commanding Regiment.

Lieut. B. H. Berry,
Acting Asst'nt Adj.-Gen.

JAMES I. CHRISTIANCY, M. H.
Lt. co. D, 9th Mich. Cavalry

CHRISTIANCY, JAMES I., Monroe.
Enlisted in co. C, Seventeenth infantry, May 28, 1862, at Monroe for three years.

Age 18.

Mustered, July 2, 1862.

Sergeant major, Aug. 26, 1862.

Commissioned 2nd lt., co. K, Dec. 28, 1862.

Commissioned 2nd lt., co. D, Ninth cavalry, Nov. 3, 1862.

Mustered, Feb. 25, 1863.

Aide-de-camp, on Gen. Custer's staff, from May, 1863 to 1865.

Severely wounded in action.

Honorally discharged at Detroit, Mich., Aug. 22, 1865. Deceased.

Medal of Honor award: — The War Department awarded the Medal of Honor to James I. Christiancy, 1st lt., co. D, 9th Mich. cavalry, Oct. 10, 1892.

Ground of award: "May 28, 1864, while acting as aide, at Hawes Shops, Va., James I. Christiancy voluntarily led a part of the line into the fight, and was twice wounded."

The following is quoted from a report of the battle made by Brigadier-General G. A. Custer, commander, to Ass't Adjt.-Gen. First Division Cavalry Corps;

"The enemy was driven from his position in great confusion compelling him to leave the ground strewn with his dead and wounded . . . The pursuit was kept up until the enemy had placed himself beyond the range of our guns. From an examination of the ground after the engagement it was ascertained that the loss of the enemy was far heavier than during any previous engagement of the same extent and duration. The havoc was particularly great in Butler's brigade of mounted infantry. Our loss was greater than in any other engagement of the camapign. . . Lieut. James I. Christiancy (one of my personal aides while gallantly

The Navy
Medal of Honor

The original
Army Medal of Honor.

The present Army Medal
of Honor.

THE MEDAL OF HONOR.

The Highest Decoration Conferred by the United States Government.

cheering on the men in the thickest of the fight and at
the moment when the tide of battle was being turned in
our favor, received two wounds, one carried away his
thumb and the other inflicting a very dangerous and
painful wound through the thigh.   At the same time
his horse was shot under him.)"

The Seventeenth Michigan was organized at Detroit
in the spring of 1862 and started for Washington, D. C.,
Aug. 27, 1862, under command of Col. William Withington of Jackson with an enrollment of 982 officers and
men.

It was assigned to First Brigade, First Division,
Ninth Army Corps.

"The field, staff and line officers follows:—(At organiza-
    tion)
    Colonel Wm. H. Withington, Jackson.
    Lieut. Col. Constant Luce, Monroe.
    Major George Collins-Lyons, Jackson.
    Surgeon Abram R. Calkins, Allegan.
    Assistant Surgeon Jonathan Beviere, Grand Rapids.
    Second Assistant Surgeon Albert Daniels, Richland.
    Adjutant Wm. V. Richards, Ann Arbor.
    Quartermaster Charles Ford, Jackson.

"The companies making up the regiment were:—
    A—Capt. L. L. Comstock, Adrian.
        1st Lieut. John S. Vreeland, Adrian.
        2nd Lieut. Richard A. Watts, Adrian.
    B—Capt. Isaac L. Clarkson, Manchester.
        1st Lieut. J. Cunningham, Detroit.
        2nd Lieut. Abraham Horton, Summit.
    C—Capt. Henry B. Androus, Coldwater.
        1st Lieut. George H. Laird, Colon.
        2nd Lieut. Wm. E. Duffield, Monroe.

D—Capt. Julius C. Burrows, Kalamazoo.
  1st Lieut. Wm. H. White, Wayland.
  2nd Lieut. Wm. S. Logan, Richland.
E—Capt. Gabriel Campbell, Ypsilanti.
  1st Lieut. Thomas Matthews, Flint.
  2nd Lieut. James T. Morgan, Muskegon.
F—Capt. Frederic W. Swift, Detroit.
  1st Lieut. John Tyler, Detroit.
  2nd Lieut. Wm. Winnegar, Grass Lake.
G—Capt. John Goldsmith, Jackson.
  1st Lieut. Rowen Summers, Jackson.
  2nd Lieut. Christian Rath, Jackson.
H—Capt. Charles A. Edmonds, Quincy.
  1st Lieut. J. P. C. Church, Jackson.
  2nd Lieut. Benj. F. Clark, Quincy.
I—Capt. Alfred Brooks, Kalamazoo.
  1st Lieut. Nelson D. Curtiss, Kalamazoo.
  2nd Lieut. George Gallifan, Kalamazoo.
J—Capt. Wm. W. Thayer, Battle Creek.
  1st Lieut. James E. Thomas, Grass Lake.
  2nd Lieut. Benj. E. Baker, Jackson.

"Perhaps no other Michigan regiment had such a serious test of its patriotism, courage and soldierly qualities so soon after arriving in the field as the Seventeenth. Scarcely two weeks from the time it left the State it participated in one of the severest battles of the war, considering the numbers engaged.

"September 14th, the 17th and 9th corps engaged the enemy at South Mountain, Md., where the corps attempted to cross the mountain through Turner's Gap and drive the Confederates from the summit, where they had taken advantage of their position behind stone fences and other obstructions and from commanding po'nts had planted their artillery to sweep the narrow roads over which the Union troops must pass.

"The 17th had been so recently organized and was so inexperienced in actual warfare that the men did not realize the desperate task they were assigned until the enemy's shot and shell were crashing through their ranks—almost at a moment's notice plunged into the horrible realities of battle. On the crest of the mountain behind stone walls the enemy awaited their advance. The orders came for the 17th to charge, when with wild cheers the regiment rushed into the storm of lead and drove the enemy from his stone defenses, and sent him retreating down the slope of the mountain. It was this charge which secured them the title of the Stonewall Regiment and honorable distinction which clung to them through the war. Out of about 500 men the regiment lost 140 killed and wounded, and so baptized, the 17th began its military career." There follows their service at Antietam, Sept. 17, 1862; Fredericksburg, Va., Dec. 12–14, 1862; siege of Vicksburg; Jackson, Miss., July 11–18, 1863; Blue Spring, Tenn., Oct. 10, 1863; London, Tenn., Nov. 14, 1863.

The troops were sent to Lenoir Station west of Knoxville to contest the advance of Gen. Longstreet then marching on Knoxville. As the Union troops fell slowly back upon Knoxville, the 17th acted as rear guard and fought a severe engagement with Longstreet's forces at Campbell's Station. During the night the Union troops fell back to Knoxville where they occupied the entrenchments of Fort Saunders, a strong earthwork. During a brilliant sortie the 17th set fire to a house occupied by rebel sharpshooters, but the light of the burning house revealed the regiment and in the furious cannonade which followed Lieut. Billingsby was killed.

The 17th occupied Fort Saunders during the siege
and helped repel the desperate charge of the enemy.
The 17th followed Gen. Longstreet to Knoxville
and into East Tenn., marching continuously, nearly
destitute of supplies, enduring hardsh:ps cheerfully,
though at times confronted by starvation and cold from
which their threadbare uniforms offered slight protection. The 17th were also engaged at Strawberry
Plains, Tenn., Wilderness, Ny River, Spottsylvania,
North Anna, Va., Bethesda Church, Va., Cold Harbor,
Petersburg, Va., the Crater, Weldon R. R., Va., Reams
Station, Poplar Spring Church, Va., Hatchers Run,
Fort Stedman, Capture of Petersburg, Siege of Petersburg.

Chas. D. Cowles in *Record of Service of Michigan
Volunteers*, Vol. XVII.

GEORGE W. CLUTE, M. H.
Corp. co. I, 14th Mich. Infantry

CLUTE, GEORGE W., (Veteran) Marathon. Enlisted
in co. I, 14th infantry, Dec. 23, 1861 at Marathon for
three years.
Age 19.
Mustered, Feb. 13, 1862.
Re-enlisted, Jan. 4, 1864 at Columbia, Tenn.
Mustered Feb. 4, 1864.
Corporal co. I, 14th Mich.
Mustered out at Louisville, Ky., July 18, 1865.
Later residence, Mt. Morris, Mich.
Medal of Honor award:—George W. Clute, corp. co.
I, 14th Mich. inf. was awarded the Medal of Honor
by the War Dept., Aug. 26, 1898.

Ground of award:—"March 19, 1865, at Bentonville, N. C. in charge captured the flag of the 40th N. C. (C. S. A.); the flag being taken in a personal encounter with an officer who carried and defended it".

GABRIEL COLE, M. H.
Corpl. co. I, 5th Mich. Cavalry

COLE, GABRIEL, Salem. Enlisted in co. I, 5th cav., Aug. 19, 1862, at Allegan, for three years.

Age 31.

Mustered, Aug. 30, 1862.

Wounded in action and left at Hanover, Pa., July 3, 1863.

Corporal.

Honorably discharged at Annapolis, Md., June 27, 1865.

Medal of Honor award:—Gabriel Cole, corpl. co. I, 5th Mich. cav., was awarded the Congressional Medal of Honor, Sept. 27, 1864 for the capture of a flag Sept. 19, 1864, at Winchester, Va.

ULRICH L. CROCKER, M. H.
Pvt. co. M, 6th Mich. Cavalry

CROCKER, ULRICH L., Vergennes. Enl'sted in co. M, 6th cav., Sept. 29, 1862, at Vergennes, for three years.

Age 18.

Mustered, Oct. 11, 1862.

Corporal, Jan. 1, 1865.

Mustered out at Fort Leavenworth, Kansas, Nov. 24, 1865.

Medal of Honor awarded by the Secretary of War for capture of Confederate battle flag at Cedar Creek, Oct. 19, 1864.

Medal of Honor award:—Ulrich L. Crocker, private, company M, 6th Mich. cav., Oct. 5, 1878, was awarded Medal of Honor for the capture of flag of the 18th Georgia (C. S. A.), at Cedar Creek, Oct. 19, 1864.

In the report submitted to Secretary of War, Edward M. Stanton, by Major Gen. Geo. M. Meade, there is a list of all the Michigan soldiers in the Civil War who have been awarded the Medal of Honor prior to Oct. 31, 1864. The Michigan men mentioned are:—

Gabriel Cole, private, 5th Mich. inf.

Henry M. Fox, sergeant, 5th Mich. cav.

Ulrich Crocker, private, 6th Mich. cav.

The above are the names of soldiers of the Army of the Potomac who have individually captured flags from the enemy since July 1, 1863 and who for their gallantry are recommended to the War department as worthy to receive Medals of Honor.

2nd Army Corps.

Sergeant Joseph B. Kemp, Co. D, 5th Mich., captured the flag of 31st N. C., tearing it from the staff which remained in the hands of the color bearer.

Corp. Benj. F. Youngs, 1st Mich. S. S., captured the colors of 35th N. C. at Petersburg, June 17, 1864.

"Over 200 flags captured from the rebels were received at the Adj. office. Many were disposed of by those capturing them not knowing that they were public property."

Hdqts. Middle Military Division.

Oct. 21, 1864.

The following named officers and enlisted men will proceed to Washington, D. C. with colors captured from the enemy in the engagement of the 19th instant and will deliver them over to the Sec't'y of War. This duty being accomplished they will immediately join their proper command.

The quartermaster's dept. will furnish necessary transportation.

Col. Geo. M. Love, 166 N. Y. Vol.

Capt. E. B. Edwards, co. A, 1st Vt. cav.

Sergt. D. H. Scofield, 5th N. Y. cav.

Sergt. E. D. Woofbury, co. E, 87 Pa. vol.

Private T. M. Wells, chief bugler, 6th N. Y. cav.

Private Ulrich Crocker, co. M, 6th Mich. cav.

Private James Sweeney, co. A, 1st Vt. cav.

Private J. Parks, co. A, 9th N. Y. cav.

Private Ira Hough, co. E, 8th Ind. vol.

(Signed) C. Kingsbury, Jr.,

Assistant Adjutant-General.

THOMAS W. CUSTER, M. H.

Lt. co. B, 6th Mich. Cavalry

CUSTER, THOMAS W., Monroe. Enlisted in company H, 21st Ohio, Sept. 2, 1861, for three years.

Age 18.

Served with this organization until Oct. 10, 1864.

Re-entered service in company B, 6th Mich. cav. as 2nd lieut.

Commissioned to date, July 11, 1864.

Brevet 1st lieutenant, captain, and major, U. S. volunteers, Mar. 13, 1865, for distinguished and gallant conduct.

Discharged at Detroit, Mich., Nov. 24, 1865.

2nd lieutenant, 1st U. S. infantry,. Feb. 23, 1866.

1st lieutenant, 7th U. S. cavalry, July 28, 1866.

Regimental quartermaster, Dec. 3, 1866.

Captain, Dec. 2, 1875.

Brevet captain to date, March 2, 1867, for gallant and distinguished conduct in the engagement with the enemy at Waynesboro, Va., March 2, 1865.

Major March 2, 1867, for distinguished conduct with the enemy at Namozine Church, Va., April, 1865.

Lieut. col. March 2, 1867, for distinguished courage and service at the battle of Sailors Creek, Va.

Medal of Honor awarded:—April 24, 1865 for the capture of a flag at Namozine Church, April 2, 1865.

A second Medal of Honor, May 22, 1865, for the capture of a flag at Sailors Creek, April 6th, 1865.

Killed in action with the Sioux Indians at Little Big River, Mont. Terr., June 25, 1876.

Lt. Custer was one of the four soldiers in the United States to receive the second award of the Medal of Honor.

Ground of award:—The War department issued a Medal of Honor to 2nd Lieut. Thos. W. Custer, co. B, 6th Mich. cavalry, May 3. Place: Namozine Church, Va. Date of action, April 2, 1865. Ground: Capture of flag.

2nd Medal of Honor given by War dept. May 26, 1865, for action April 6, 1865 at Sailors Creek, Va. "Leaped his horse over the enemy's works and captured two stands of colors having his horse shot under him and receiving a severe wound."

Gen. Geo. A. Custer, brigadier general of Michigan volunteers in an order addressed to his troops dated April 9, 1865 said:—"During the past six months, though in most instances confronted by superior numbers, you have captured from the enemy in open battle 111 pieces of field artillery, 65 battle flags and upward of 10,000 prisoners of war, including seven general officers. Within the past ten days and included in the above you have captured 46 field pieces of artillery and 37 battle flags. You have never lost a gun, never lost a color, never been defeated, and notwithstanding the numerous engagements in which you have borne a prominent part you have captured every piece of artillery which the enemy has opened upon you."

Thomas Ward Custer, brother of General G. A. Custer, born in New Rumley, Harrison county, Ohio, March 15, 1845.

Died in Mont., June 25, 1876.

Enlisted in Ohio regiment as aide-de-camp on Gen. G. A. Custer staff, Army of Potomac.

2nd Lt. in 6th cavalry, Nov. 8, 1864.

His horse was often neck and neck with that of his famous brother. When he captured his second flag at Sailors Creek, he was shot by the standard bearer in the face. He was preparing to charge again when he was stopped by his brother and told to go to the rear. As he paid no attention to this request it became necessary for Gen. Custer to order him under arrest before he could check his ardor.

In the spring of 1865 he accompanied Gen. Custer to Texas and served on the staff until mustered out in Nov. He received the brevets of captain, major, and lieutenant colonel, Feb. 23, 1866; 2nd lieut. in 1st infantry of regular army and on July 28, 1st lieut. in

brother's reg. of 7th cav.   When asked his opinion of
his brother Gen. Custer said:—"If you want to know
my opinion of Tom, I can only say that I think he
should be the general and I the captain."

"1st Lieut. Thos. W. Custer, 6th Mich. cav. to be
major of vol. by brevet for distinguished conduct at
the battles of Dinwiddie Court House, March 31; Five
Forks, April 1; Sailors Creek, April 6, 1865 at which
latter place he leaped his horse over the enemy's works,
be ng one of the first to enter them and captured two
stands of colors having his horse shot under him and
received a severe wound."

Order signed by Maj. P. H. Sheridan.

BYRON M. CUTCHEON, M. H.
Major 20th Michigan Infantry

CUTCHEON, BYRON M.   Born at Pembroke, N. H.,
    May 11, 1836.
Educated in Pembroke preparatory schools; Mich.
    State Normal, Ypsilanti; was graduated from U.
    of M., classical course, 1861, and the law school in
    1866.
Came to Michigan 1855.
Principal of Ypsilanti high school.
Served in Civil War with the 20th, 27th Mich. inf.;
    commanded 2nd brigade, first division, Army of
    Potomac, in 1864; mustered out, 1865.
Practiced law at Manistee, where he began in 1867.
Presidential elector, 1868.
City attorney of Manistee, 1870–'71; prosecuting
    attorney, 1873–'74; Postmaster. 1877–'83.
Regent of University of Michigan, 1875–'83.
President, orator and poet of Alumni Association, U,
    of M,

Member of forty-eighth, forty-ninth and fiftieth congresses.

Member of Sons of American Revolution; Medal of Honor Legion, G. A. R.

Author of "Memoirs of Gen. Phil H. Sheridan," 1891; "History of the class of 1861, U. of M.," 1902; "History of the 20th Mich. infantry," 1904; joint author, "History of Michigan as a Province Territory and State," 1906.

Later residence, 74 Paris Ave., Grand Rapids.

Died, 1908.

Military record:—Cutcheon, Byron M.—Ypsilanti. Entered service in company O, 20th infantry, at organization, as second lieutenant, for three years. Age 26.

Commissioned, July 15, 1862. Mustered, July 15, 1862.

Commissioned captain, July 29, 1862. Mustered, Aug. 16, 1862.

Commissioned major, Oct. 14, 1862.

Commissioned lieut. colonel, Nov. 16, 1863. Mustered to date Nov. 16, 1863.

Commissioned colonel, Nov. 21, 1863. Mustered, Jan. 8, '64.

Wounded in action, May 10, '64.

Commanding second brigade, first division, Ninth army corps, from Oct. 17, 1864 to Dec., 1864.

Twice wounded at Spottsylvania Court House.

Brevet colonel U. S. volunteers, Aug. 18, 1864, for gallant services at battles of Wilderness and Spottsylvania, and operations before Petersburg, Va.

Mustered out, Dec. 18, 1864.

Commissioned colonel 27th inf., Nov. 12, 1864.

Mustered, Dec. 19, 1864.

Commanding second brigade, Jan. and Feb., 1865.

Resigned and honorably discharged, March 6, 1865, by S. O. No. 100 War dept.

Brevet brigadier gen. volunteers, March 13, 1865, for conspicuous bravery at battle of Wilderness, Va.

Medal of Honor by Congress, June 29, 1891, for conspicuous bravery at Horseshoe Bend, Ky., May 10, 1863.

Medal of Honor award:—Byron Cutcheon, major 20th Michigan inf., awarded Congressional Medal of Honor, June 29, 1891.

Place:—Horseshoe Bend, Ky.

Time:—May 10, 1863.

Ground of award:—"Distinguished gallantry in leading his regiment in a charge on a house occupied by enemy."

CHARLES H. DE PUY, M. H.
Sergt. co. H, 1st Mich. S. S.

DE PUY, CHARLES H.   Enlisted in battery D, First Ill. light artillery, Aug. 17, 1861 at Lima, Ind.

Discharged for disability, Feb. 10, 1863.

Re-entered service in co. H, 1st Mich. S. S., Aug. 5, 1863 at Lima for three years.

Age 21.

Mustered Aug. 20, 1863.

Taken prisoner, July 30, 1864.

Promoted sergeant, July 2, 1864.

Confined at Danville, N. C., July, 1864 to Feb. 20, 1865.

Discharged at Alexandria, Va., July 7. 1865.

Later residence, Kalkaska, Mich.

July 30, 1896, Charles H. De Puy was awarded a
Medal of Honor by Congress for gallantry in action,
July 30, 1864, at Petersburg, Va.
Ground of award:—"Being an old artillerist aided Gen-
eral Bartlett in working the guns of the dismantled
fort."

Report 205 by Col. Chas. V. DeLand, 1st Mich.
sharpshooters.
"July 30, 1864.
Captain:—The participation of this regiment in the
action is hereby stated as follows:—We went into the
action with about 100 guns. In the charge on the
enemy's works the regiment took a small section on
the left of the fort capturing about 30 prisoners in
their works. The command aided in repulsing two
charges and also in clearing a small flanker of rebels,
capturing about 20 more, making about 50 in all. A
part of the regiment under the orders of Gen. Bartlett,
assisted in working two pieces of cannon found near
the fort as long as ammunition could be obtained, then
the works were abandoned. We lost a large number of
prisoners and one State color."

Concerning the lost colors:—
Aug. 3, 1864.
Report by Lieut. Col. Byron M. Cutcheon,
Commanding 20th Mich. inf.
After describing the stampede of the 46th N.Y. and
gallantry and coolness of the sharpshooters, Cutcheon
says:—"It was sometime before I learned that any
part of my command was still in the rebel fort, but I
learned at about three p. m. that our colors were still
flying on their works, defended by about 30 of our men.

Of these about ten escaped and the remainder were taken, among them all that remained of the color guard, of whom only two remained uninjured. So far as I can learn the colors of the 20th and the 2nd Mich. were the last displayed on the rebel fort."

ROBERT DODD, M. H.
Pvt. co. E, 27th Mich. Infantry

DODD, Robert. Hamtramck. Enlisted with Stanton Guard, May 4, 1862.
At Detroit for 3 years.
Age 18.
Mustered, May 6, 1862.
Mustered out at Detroit, Mich., Sept. 25, 1862.
Re-entered service.
Enlisted in company E, 27th infantry, as corporal, Nov. 19, 1862.
At Detroit for 3 years.
Mustered, Feb. 25, 1863.
Mustered out at DeLaney House, D. C., July 26, 1865.
Medal of Honor award:—Dodd, Robert F., priv. co. E, 27th Mich. inf., Hamtramck, July 27, 1896, was awarded Medal of Honor, July 30, 1864, at Petersburg, Va.
Ground of award:—While acting as orderly voluntarily assisted to carry off the wounded from the ground in front of the crater while exposed to heavy fire.

JOHN A. FALCONER, M. H.
Corp. co. A, 17th Mich. Infantrv

FALCONER, JOHN A., Manchester. Enlisted in co. A, 17th inf., June 27, 1862, at Manchester, for three years.

Age 18.

Mustered, Aug. 19, 1862.

Corporal, March 1, 1864.

Sergeant, May 12, 1865.

Mustered out at DeLaney House, D. C., June 3, 1865.

Received Medal of Honor for gallantry at Ft. Saunders, Tenn.

Later residence, Warnersburg, Mo.

Medal of Honor award:—To John A. Falconer, corp. co. A, 17th Mich. inf., July 27, 1896, by War Department for gallantry at Fort Saunders, Knoxville, Tenn., where on the 20th of Nov., 1863, he "conducted the burning party of his regiment at the time a charge was made on the enemy's picket line, and burned the house which sheltered the enemy's sharpshooters, thus insuring success to a hazardous enterprise."

CHARLES S. FALL, M. H.

Serg. co. E, 26th Mich. Infantry

FALL, CHARLES S., Hamburg. Enlisted in co. E, 26th inf., Aug. 6, 1862, at Hamburg for three years.

Age 20.

Mustered, Sept. 10, 1862.

Corporal, March 28, 1863.

1st Sergeant, Sept. 1, 1864.

Sergeant major, Jan. 18, 1865.

Mustered out at Alexandria, Va., June 4, 1865.

Medal of Honor:—Awarded by Congress to Charles S. Fall, Serg. co. E, 26th Mich. inf., May 13, 1899 for conspicuous gallantry at Spottsylvania C. H., Va., on the 12th of May, 1864, for being "One of the first to mount the Confederate works where he bayonetted two of the enemy and captured a Confederate flag but threw it away to continue the pursuit of the enemy."

"The 26th was organized at Jackson and mustered into service Dec. 12, 1862. The field staff and line officers at organization were as follows:—Col. Judson S. Farrar, Mt. Clemens; Lt. Col. Henry H. Wells, Detroit; Maj. William Donnel, Saginaw; Surgeon Ennis Church, Marshall; Assistant Surgeon Mahlon H. Raymond, Grass Lake; 2nd Ass't Surgeon Odney D. Broods, Muskegon; Adjutant Chas. D. Fox, Lyons; Quartermaster Charles E. Crane, Adrian; Chaplain Jonathan Blanchard, Ann Arbor."

Co. C—Capt. James A. Lothian, Muskegon; 1st Lt. Henry Dopson, Muskegon; 2nd Lt. Chauncey Gibbs, Muskegon.

Co. E—Capt. John C. Colver, Hamburg; 1st Lt. Edwin Hadley, Ann Arbor; 2nd Lt. Charles E. Grisson, Hamburg.

"The regiment left Jackson for Washington the day after it was mustered into service and was immediately assigned to provost duty at Alexandria, Va.

"In April, 1863, the 26th proceeded to Suffolk and from this point joined in several expeditions in which it gave evidence of its future splendid record.

"In July it was ordered to N. Y. City during the excitement of the riots attending the draft.

"In October it joined the Army of the Potomac, 1st brigade, first division, second corps, General Miles and Gen. Hancock."

Had reputation of being the best skirmish regiment in the army and so took part in many hazardous advances.

"On the 11th of May the 26th gallantly attacked the enemy across the river Potomac. The next day it participated in the historic charge, near Spottsylvania, upon the Confederate works, which were carried at the

point of the bayonet in a hand to hand struggle. The
26th being one of the first regiments to plant its colors
on the rebel works. Jumping over the works, a battery
of two guns with the gunners were captured but the
regiment swept along the enemy's lines for a mile
taking a large number of prisoners, guns and colors but
suffered severely from the terrific fire of the enemy.
This charge was made by the 26th after an all night's
march in a storm reaching its position in the line to
make the assault just as the Union lines moved forward in the charge."
Disbanded, June 16, 1865.

ALEXANDER A. FORMAN, M. H.
Corp. co. E, 7th Mich. Infantry

FORMAN, ALEXANDER A., Jonesville. Enlisted in co.
   C, 7th inf., as corporal, June 19, 1861, at Jonesville,
   for 3 years.
Age 19.
Mustered Aug. 22, 1861.
Wounded in action at Fair Oaks, Va., May 31, 1862.
Discharged for disability at Detroit, Nov. 10, 1862.
Medal of Honor award:—Alexander A. Forman, corp.
   co. E, 7th Mich. inf., was awarded Medal of Honor by
   Congress, Aug. 17, 1895.
Place:—Fair Oaks, Va.
Time:—May 31, 1862.
Ground of award:—Although wounded he continued
   fighting until faint from the loss of blood, he was
   carried off from the field.

HENRY M. FOX, M. H.

Sergt. co. M, 5th Mich. Cavalry

Fox, HENRY M., Union.   Enlisted in company M, 5th
cav., Aug. 12, 1862, at Coldwater, for 3 years.
Age 16.
Mustered, Aug. 30, 1862.
Promoted corp'l, Aug. 2, 1863; 1st sergeant, Jan. 1,
1865; 2nd lt., April 4, 1865.
Mustered out at Fort Leavenworth, Kan., June 19,
1865.
Later residence, Union, Mich.
Medal of Honor award:—Sept. 27, 1864, for capture of
a flag, Sept. 19, 1864, at Winchester, Va.

SAMUEL S. FRENCH, M. H.

7th Mich. Infantry

FRENCH, SAMUEL S., (Veteran), Tuscola county.
Enlisted in co. E, 7th Mich. inf., Aug. 12, 1861, at
Tuscola, for 3 years.
Age 20.
Mustered, Aug. 22, 1861.
Re-enlisted, Dec. 18, 1863, at Stevensburg, Va.
Mustered, Dec. 19, 1863.
Wounded in action, at Fair Oaks, Va., May 31, 1862.
Corporal.
Absent sick, Dec. 14, 1864.
Medal of Honor award:—Conferred by Congress, Oct.
24, 1895, for bravery, May 31, 1862, at Fair Oaks—
"Continued fighting after being wounded until he
fainted from loss of blood."

HAROLD A. FURLONG, M. H.
Lieut. 353rd Infantry, 89th Division

FURLONG, HAROLD ARTHUR, Detroit.
Born Aug. 1, 1895.
Son of Arthur D. and Myrtle A. Furlong.
Educated in public schools of Pontiac and Saginaw,
Michigan, and Springfield, Illinois. Was graduated
from Saginaw high school; attended M. A. C. three
years, specializing in dairy chemistry.
Military training at Ft. Sheridan, Ill. and Camp Funston, Kansas; is the first Michigan man in the World's
war to be awarded the Medal of Honor.
Military record:—Enlisted at Detroit, Mich., May 10,
1917, in 9th co., 10 Prov. training regiment,
Ft. Sheridan. Commissioned second lieut. at Ft.
Sheridan. Transferred to Camp Funston as special
instructor in physical drill and bayonet practice;
transferred to co. M, 353rd inf., 89th division, with
which he went overseas, May 22, 1918. Promoted
first lieut., Oct., 1918 in the field. Fought in three
engagements in St. Mihiel sector, France. With
third army of occupation near Coblenz, Germany,
Feb., 1919. Awarded the Distinguished Service
Cross by Major General Winn, commander of the
89th division at Gondelshien, Germany, Dec. 17,
1918 for extraordinary bravery in action, Nov. 1,
1918.
Medal of Honor award:—For conspicuous gallantry
and intrepidity above and beyond the call of duty
in action with the enemy near Bantheville, France,
Nov. 1, 1918. Immediately after the opening of the
attack in Bois de Bantheville, when his company
was held up by severe machine-gun fire from the

front, which killed his company commander and
several soldiers, Lieut. Furlong moved out in advance
of the line with great courage and coolness; crossing
an open space several hundred yards wide and taking
up a position behind the line of machine-guns, he
closed in on them, one at a time, killing a number of
the enemy with his rifle, putting four machine-gun
nests out of action and driving twenty German prisoners into our lines.

Home address:—Arthur D. Furlong, 2950 West Grand
Boulevard, Detroit.

By direction of President Woodrow Wilson, under
the provisions of Act of Congress approved July 9,
1918, the Medal of Honor was awarded Feb. 5th, 1919,
on the recommendation cabled by Gen. Pershing.

CORNELIUS HADLEY, M. H.
Serg. co. F, 9th Mich. Calvary

HADLEY, CORNELIUS, Litchfield. Enlisted in co. H.,
4th inf., as corporal, June 20, 1861, at Adrian, for 3
years.

Age 23.

Mustered, June 20, 1861.

Sergeant.

Discharged for disability at Philadelphia, Pa., Oct.
23, 1862.

Re-entered service. Enlisted in co. M, 9th cav., as
sergeant, May 7, 1863, at Coldwater, for 3 years.

Mustered, May 19, 1863.

Transferred to co. F, May 20, 1863.

Discharged to accept commission in U. S. colored troops,
June 16, 1864.

Died March 22, 1902.

Buried at Litchfield.

Medal of Honor award:—Medal of Honor awarded by
the War department to Cornelius Hadley, sergeant
co. F, 9th Mich. cav., on the fifth of April, 1898.

Ground of award:—Nov. 20, 1863, at Knoxville,
Tenn., with one companion voluntarily carried
through the enemy's lines important dispatches from
General Grant to General Burnsides, then besieged
within Knoxville, and brought back replies. His
comrade's horse being shot and the man taken prisoner.

SIDNEY HAIGHT, M. H.
Corp. co. E, 1st Mich. S. S.

HAIGHT, SIDNEY. Goodland. Enlisted in co. E, 1st
Michigan sharpshooters, Oct. 23, 1863, at Goodland,
for 3 years.

Age 17.

Mustered, Oct. 30, 1863.

Corporal.

Mustered out at Delaney House, D. C., July 28, 1865.

Medal of Honor award:—Sidney Haight, corp. co.
E, 1st Mich. S. S., was awarded Congressional Medal
of Honor, July 31, 1896.

Ground of award:—July 30, 1864, at Petersburg, Va.,
"Instead of retreating, remained in the captured
works, regardless of his personal safety and exposed
to firing, which he boldly and deliberately returned
until the enemy was upon him."

SMITH HASTINGS, M. H.
Capt. co. M, 5th Mich. Cavalry

HASTINGS, SMITH. Enlisted in co. C, 1st inf., April 24.
1861, at Coldwater, for 3 mo.

Age 18.

Mustered May 1, 1861. Mustered out at Detroit, Aug. 7, 1861.

Re-entered service in co. M, 5th cav., as 1st Lieut. at organization.

Commissioned, Aug. 14, 1862. Mustered. Aug. 30, 1862.

Commissioned captain, Jan. 10, 1863. Wounded in action at Trevilian Station, Va., June 12, 1864.

Commissioned major, Aug. 9, 1864. Mustered, Sept. 20, 1864.

Commissioned colonel, Dec. 17, 1864.

Commissioned lt. colonel, Nov. 10, 1864. Mustered, Dec. 31, 1864.

Mustered out at Ft. Leavenworth, Kan., June 22, 1865.

Later residence, Denver, Colo.

Medal of Honor award:—Smith H. Hastings, Captain co. M, 5th Mich. cav., was awarded Congressional Medal of Honor, Aug. 2, 1897. Action, July 24, 1863. Newby's Crossroads, Va.

Ground of award:—While in command of a squadron in rear guard of a cavalry division—then retiring before the advance of a corps of infantry—was attacked by the enemy and orders having been given to abandon the guns of a section of field artillery with the rear guard that were in imminent danger of capture, he disregarded orders received and aided in repelling the attack and saving the guns.

EDWARD HILL, M. H.
Capt. co. K, 16th Mich. Infantry

HILL, EDWARD. Detroit. Entered service in co. D, lancers, at organization as 1st lt., Oct. 16, 1861; at Detroit, for 3 years. Mustered out, Mar. 20, '62.

Re-entered service, co. K, 16th inf., at organization, as 2nd lt.

Commissioned, Mar. 19, 1862. Mustered, Mar. 24, 1862.

Commissioned 1st lt., July 29, 1862. Mustered, July 29, 1862.

Wounded in action at Manassas, Va., Aug. 30, 1862.

Commissioned captain co. H, April 17, 1863. Mustered, May 24, 1863.

Transferred to co. K, Oct. 1, 1863.

Wounded in action, June 1, 1864.

Commissioned major, Sept. 30, 1864. Mustered, Jan. 17, 1865.

Discharged to accept promotion, May 11, 1865.

Commissioned lt. col., May 8, 1865. Mustered, May 11, 1865.

Division inspector, June, 1865.

Discharged at Jeffersonville, Ind., July 1, 1865.

Medal of Honor award:—Medal of Honor conferred by Congress, Dec. 14, 1893, for "distinguished gallantry in action at Cold Harbor, Va., June, '64."

Ground of award:—"Led the brigade skirmish line in a desperate charge on the enemy's masked batteries to the muzzles of the guns, where he was severely wounded." "June 1, 1864. Cold Harbor."

ADDISON J. HODGES, M. H.
Co. B, 47th Ohio Infantry

HODGES, ADDISON J. Enlisted in co. B, 47th Ohio inf., June 15, 1861, for 3 yrs.

Age 20.

Promoted corporal.

Discharged, at East Point, Ga., Sept. 26, 1864.

Medal of Honor award:—Dec. 31, 1907.   Addison J.
  Hodges, pvt., co. B, 47th Ohio inf., was awarded a
  Medal of Honor by Congress.
Place of action:—Vicksburg, Miss.
Time of action:—May 3, 1863.
Ground of award:—"Was one of a party that volun-
  teered and attempted to run the enemy's batteries
  with a steam tug and two barges loaded with sub-
  sistence stores."
[47th Ohio infantry.
  Co. B was organized by W. H. Ward of Adrian, Mich.
  There being no vacancy in Michigan, its services
  were offered to Governor of Ohio, who assigned it to
  the 47th Ohio.]

JOHN HACK, M. H.
Co. B, 47th Ohio Infantry

HACK, JOHN.   Enlisted ın co. B, 47th Ohio inf., June
  15, 1861, at Adrian, for 3 yrs.
Age 18.
Discharged at expiration of term of service, at Atlanta,
  Ga., Aug. 20, 1864.
Medal of Honor award:—Date of award, Feb. 5, 1907.
Place of action:—Vicksburg, Miss., May 3, 1865.
Ground of award:—"Was one of a party of volunteers
  who attempted to run the enemy's batteries with a
  steam tug and two barges loaded with subsistence
  stores."

CHARLES M. HOLTON, M. H.
7th Mich. Cavalry

HOLTON, CHARLES M., 1st sergeant, co. A, 7th Mich.
  cav., Battle Creek.   Enlisted in co. A, 7th Mich.
  cav., as 1st sergeant, Sept. 4, 1862, at Battle Creek,
  for 3 years.

Age 24.

Mustered, Oct. 13, 1862.

Discharged to accept promotion, May 1, 1864.

Commiss·oned 2nd lt. co. C to date March 22, 1864.

Commissioned 1st lt., May 24, 1865. Mustered, May 24, 1865.

Discharged, June 17, 1865.

Medal of Honor award:—July 14, 1863, Charles M. Holton, 1st sergeant, co. A, 7th Mich. cav.

Ground of award:—Captured the flag of the 55th Va. inf. (C. S. A.). The Medal of Honor was awarded Mar. 21, 1889.

PATRICK IRWIN, M. H.
Serg. co. H, 14th Mich. Infantry

IRWIN, PATRICK (Veteran), Ann Arbor. Enlisted in co. H, 14th Mich. inf., as sergeant, Sept. 30, 1861 at Ann Arbor, for 3 years.

Age 22.

Mustered, Jan. 7, 1862.

Re-enlisted, Jan. 4, 1864, at Columbia, Tenn. Mustered, Feb. 4, 1864.

First sergeant. Discharged to accept promotion, Oct. 4, 1864.

Commissioned 2nd lt., Aug. 10, 1864. Mustered, Oct. 5, 1864.

Discharged to accept promotion, May 25, 1865.

Commissioned 1st lt. co. G, Feb. 10, 1865. Mustered, May 26, 1865.

Commissioned captain co. K, July 5, 1865.

Mustered out, July 8, 1865.

Later residence, Ann Arbor.

Medal of Honor award:—First Sergeant Patrick Irwin, veteran of co. H, 14th Mich. inf., April 28, 1896.

round of award:—Sept. 1, 1864, at Jonesboro, Ga. "In a charge by the 14th Mich. inf. against the intrenched enemy was the first man over the line of works of the enemy and demanded and received the surrender of a Confederate general officer and his command."

JOSEPH S. KEEN, M. H.
Serg. co. D, 13th Mich. Infantry

KEEN, JOSEPH S. Wayne.
Born at Stanford, Vale of Berkshire, England.
Educated in public schools of the United States.
Married Sarah W. Dean, Oct. 6, 1868.
Children: Williston A. Keen and Albert Sidney Keen.
Residence, [1918], Detroit.
Military service: Joseph S. Keen enlisted in co. D,
    13th inf.', Feb. 1, 1862, at Detroit, for three years.
Age 19.
Mustered, Feb. 27, 1862.
Corporal, August 31, 1862.
Sergeant, April 1, 1863.
Taken prisoner at Chickamauga, Ga., Sept. 30, 1863.
Returned to regiment, Oct. 1, 1864, at Atlanta, Ga.
Discharged at expiration of term of service, at Detroit,
    Feb. 28, 1865.
Medal of Honor award: Joseph S. Keen, sergeant co.
    D, 13th Mich. inf. was awarded Medal of Honor,
    Aug. 4, 1899.
Ground of award: "While on Oct. 1, 1864, an escaped
    prisoner of war within the Confederate lines, wit-
    nessed an important movement of the enemy and
    at great personal risk made his way through the
    lines with the news of the movement to Sherman's
    army."

Ed. note:—A grandson, Howard A. Keen, b. 1897, was in
service with the 17th regular field artillery in Euro-
pean war.

ANDREW J. KELLY, M. H.
17th Mich. Infantry

KELLY, ANDREW J., Adrian.   Enlisted in co. E, 17th
inf., Aug. 12, 1862, at Ypsilanti, for 3 years.
Age 18.
Mustered, Aug. 19, 1862, corp. Sergt., May 1, 1865.
Mustered out at DeLaney House, D. C., June 3, 1865.
Later residence, Crookston, Minn.
Medal of Honor award:—Received Medal of Honor
awarded by the War department, April 17, 1900 to
Private Kelly for gallantry at Knoxville, Tenn.
Ground of award:—Andrew J. Kelly, private in co. E,
17th Mich. inf. on Nov. 20, 1863, at Knoxville,
Tenn., having voluntarily accompanied a small
party to destroy buildings within the enemy's lines,
whence sharpshooters had been firing, disregarded
an order to retire, remained and completed the firing
of the buildings thus insuring their total destruction
at the imminent risk of his life from the fire of the
advancing enemy.

JOSEPH B. KEMP, M. H.
Sergt. co. D, 5th Mich. Infantry

KEMP, JOSEPH B., Veteran.   Whitmore Lake.   Enlisted in co. F, 5th inf., Aug. 19, 1861, at Ft. Wayne,
for 3 yrs.
Age 18.
Mustered, Aug. 28, 1861.

1st sergt.

Wounded in action at Gettysburg, Pa., July 2, 1863.

Re-enlisted, Jan. 22, 1864 at Ft. Wayne.

Mustered, Jan. 22, 1864.

Transferred to co. D, June 10, 1864.

Missing in action, June 22, 1864.

Commissioned 1st lt., June 10, 1864.

Mustered, July 1, 1864.

Commissioned captain co. C, May 18, 1865. Mustered, May 17, 1865.

Brevet capt. U. S. vol., April 9, 1865, for gallant and meritorious service during the campaign terminating with the surrender of the insurgent army under Gen. R. E. Lee. Mustered out at Jeffersonville, Ind., July 5, 1865.

Medal of Honor award:—1st sergt. co. D, 5th Mich. infantry, June 22, 1899.

Ground of award:—May 6, 1864, captured flag of the 31 N. C. (C. S. A.) at Wilderness, Va.

HENRY LEWIS, M. H.
Co. B, 47th Ohio Infantry

Lewis, Henry. Veteran. Enlisted in co. B, 47th Ohio inf., June 15, 1861, for 3 years. (A company organized by William H. Ward at Adrian and assigned to the 47th Ohio inf.)

Age 19.

Promoted corporal, Sept. 1, 1862.

Re-enlisted, Feb. 20, 1864, at Cleveland, Tenn. Mustered, Mar. 6, 1864.

Taken prisoner at Atlanta, Ga., July 22, 1865.

1st sergeant, Aug. 1, 1865.

Mustered out at Little Rock, Ark., Aug. 11, 1865.

Medal of Honor award:—The Congressional Medal of
Honor was conferred, April 17, 1917, on Henry
Lewis, corp. co. B, 47th Ohio inf.
Ground of award:—"For gallantry in action at Vicks-
burg, Miss., May 3, 1863."

MOSES A. LUCE, M. H.
Sergt. co. E, 4th Mich. Infantry

LUCE, MOSES A. McDonough, Ill. Enlisted in co.
E, 4th inf, June 20, 1861, at Adrian, for 3 yrs.
Age 22.
Mustered, June 20, 1861.
Sergeant, Jan. 1, 1863.
Mustered out at expiration of service, at Detroit,
June 28, 1864.
Medal of Honor award:—Awarded by Congress, Feb.
7, 1895 to Sergt. Moses A. Luce, co. E, 4th Mich.
inf. "At Laurel Hill, Va., May 10, 1864, volun-
tarily returned in the face of the advancing enemy
to the assistance of a wounded and helpless comrade,
and carried him at imminent peril to a place of
safety."

DANIEL M'FALL, M. H.
Sergt. co. E, 17th Mich. Infantry

McFALL, DANIEL, Augusta. Enlisted in co. E, 17th
inf., Aug. 6, 1862, at Ypsilanti, for 3 years.
Age 26.
Mustered, Aug. 19, 1862. Corporal. Sergeant.
Mustered out at DeLaney House, D. C., June 3, 1865.
Later residence, Cone, Mich.

Medal of Honor award:—July 27, 1896, for gallantry in
service, May 12, 1864, at Spottsylvania, Va., Medal
of Honor presented by War department to Daniel
McFall, sergeant of co. E, 17th Mich. inf. for conspicuous bravery at Spottsylvania, Va., where on
May 12, 1864, "he captured the colonel commanding
the Confederate brigade that charged the Union
batteries; on the same day rescued an officer of his
regiment from the enemy."

ALEXANDER U. M'HALE, M. H.
Corp. co. C, 26th Mich. Infantry

McHale, Alexander U., Muskegon.   Enlisted in co.
C, 26th Mich. inf., Aug. 15, 1862, at Muskegon for
3 yrs.,
Age 20.
Mustered. Sept. 15, 1862.
Corp., May 12, 1864.
Sergeant, May 13, 1865.
Commissioned 2nd lt., June 9, 1865.
Mustered out at Alexandria, Va., June 4, 1865.
Medal of Honor award:—Jan. 11, 1900, to Alexander
U. McHale, corp. co. C, 26th Mich. inf. for con-
spicuous gallantry, May 12, 1864, at Spottsylvania
Court House, Va.   "Captured a Confederate flag in
a charge, threw the flag over in front of the works
and continued in the charge on the enemy."

ALEXANDER MACOMB
Commander-in-Chief of the Army at Plattsburg

Macomb, Alexander, born in Detroit, Mich., April 3,
1782.

COMMEMORATIVE MEDAL OF HONOR
Presented to General Alexander Macomb.

Entered the army as cornet, light dragoons, Jan. 10, 1799; (N. Y.).

2nd leut. Mar. 2, 1799.

Hon. idischarged, June 15, 1800.

2nd lt. 2nd inf., Feb. 16, 1801.

1st lieut. engineers, Oct. 12, 1802.

Captain, June 11, 1805.

Maj., Feb. 23, 1808.

Lieut. col., July 23, 1811.

Col. artillery, July 6, 1812.

Brig. gen., Jan. 24, 1814. Retained as col. chief engineers, June 1, 1821.

Maj. gen., May 24, 1828.

Commander-in-chief of the army at Plattsburg, May 29, to June 25, 1841.

Brevet major general, Sept. 11, 1814, for distinguished and gallant conduct in defeating the enemy at Plattsburg, N. Y.

Commemorative Medal of Honor award:—By resolution of Congress, Nov. 3, 1814, was "Resolved that the thanks of Congress be, and they are hereby, presented to Major Gen. Macomb and through him to the officers and men of the regular army under his command and to the militia and volunteers of New York and Vermont for their gallantry and good conduct in defeating the enemy at Plattsburg, Sept. 11, repelling with 1,500 men aided by a body of militia and volunteers from N. Y. and Vermont a British veteran army greatly superior in numbers; and that the Pres. of the U. S. be requested to cause a gold medal to be struck emblematical of this triumph and presented to Major General Macomb."

Died, June 25, 1841.

JOHN W. MENTER, M. H.
Sergt. Co. D, 5th Mich. Infantry

MENTER, JOHN W. (Veteran), Superior.   Enlisted in
    co. F, 5th inf., Aug. 9, 1861, for 3 yrs.
Age 23.
Mustered, Aug. 28, 1861.
Re-enlisted, as corporal, at Brandy Station, Va., Dec.
    15, 1863.
Mustered, Dec. 27, 1863.
Transferred to co. D, June 10, 1864.
Sergeant, Feb., 1865.
Mustered out at Jeffersonville, Ind., July 5, 1865.
Later residence, Ovid, Mich.
Medal of Honor award:—John W. Menter, sergeant,
    co. D, 5th Mich. inf., April 6, 1865; capture of flag.
    Awarded May 10, 1865.

WALTER MUNDELL, M. H.
Corp. co. E, 5th Mich. Infantry

MUNDELL, WALTER, (Veteran).   Grand Rapids.   En-
    listed in co. D, 3rd inf., May 13, 1861, at Grand
    Rapids, for 3 yrs.
Age 22.
Mustered, June 10, 1861.
Taken prisoner at Fair Oaks, Va., June 1, 1862.
Returned to regiment, Nov. 20, 1862.
Re-enlisted, Dec. 23, 1863 at Brandy Station, Va.
Mustered, Dec. 23, 1863.
Transferred to co. E, 5th inf., June 10, 1864, as corp.
    Mustered out at Jeffersonville, Va., July 5, 1865.
    ied at Fowler, Mich., April 20, 1900.
Medal of Honor award:—Awarded, May 10, 1865 when
    corp. co. E, 5th Mich. inf., for capture of flag at
    Sailors Creek, April 6, 1865.

HENRY H. NASH, M. H.
Co. B, 47th Ohio Infantry

NASH, HENRY H.   Adrian.   Enlisted in co. B, 47th
  Ohio, June 15, 1861, for 3 yrs.
Age 19.
Promoted corporal.
Taken prisoner at Atlanta, Ga., July 22, 1864.
Discharged at expiration of term of service at Atlanta,
  Ga., Aug. 20, 1864.
Medal of Honor award:—Henry Nash, corpl., co. B,
  47th Ohio inf., on the 9th of March, 1909, was
  awarded a Medal of Honor by Congress.
Place of action:—Vicksburg, Miss., May 3, 1863.—
  "Was one of a party that volunteered and attempted
  to run the enemy batteries with a steam tug and two
  barges loaded with subsistence stores."

CONRAD NOLL, M. H.
Sergt. co. D, 20th Mich. infantry

NOLL, CONRAD.   Ann Arbor.   Enlisted in co. D, 20th
  inf., Aug. 11, 1862, at Ann Arbor, for three yrs.
Age 26.
Mustered, Aug. 18, 1862.
Corporal, Dec. 25, 1862.   Sergeant, Jan. 1, 1865.
Discharged, July 14, 1865, at Harper Hospital, Detroit,
  on account of wounds received in action beforePeters-
  burg, Va., July 30, 1864.
Participated in the battles: Fredericksburg, Va.;
  Horsehoe Bend, Ky.; Jackson, Miss.; Vicksburg,
  Miss.; Blue Springs; Siege of Knoxville; The Wilder-
  ness; Spottsylvania; North Anna; Cold Harbor;
  before Petersburg, June 17 and 18, 1864, July 30, '64.

Later residence, Ann Arbor.

Medal of Honor award:—Conrad Noll, sergt. co. D, 20th Mich. inf., was awarded Medal of Honor, July 28, 1896, for bravery in action at Spottsylvania, Va., May 12, 1864. "Seized the colors, the color-bearer having been shot, and gallantly fought his way out with them though the enemy was on the left flank and rear."

ELLIOTT M. NORTON, M. H.
Lt. co. H, 6th Mich. Cavalry

NORTON, ELLIOTT M., Wayland. Enlisted in co. B, 6th Mich. cav., Nov. 21, 1862, at Grand Rapids for 3 yrs.

Age 27.

Mustered, Dec. 4, 1862.

Sergeant, April 1, 1863.

Sergeant major, Aug. 6, 1864.

Discharged to accept promotion, Aug. 6, 1864.

Commissioned 2nd lieut, co. H, to date, July 1, 1864.

Mustered, Aug. 7, 1864.

Discharged to accept promotion, Jan. 29, 1865.

Commissioned 1st lieut. and adjutant to date, Jan. 4, 1865.

Mustered, Jan. 29, 1865.

Transferred to 1st cav., Nov., 1865.

Mustered out at Salt Lake City, Utah, Mar. 10, 1866.

Medal of Honor award:—Conferred by War dep't on Elliott M. Norton, 2nd lieut. co. H, 6th Mich. cav. Issued May 3, 1865, for the capture of two flags, on the 6th of April, 1865, at Sailors Creek, Va.

JOHN R. NORTON, M. H.
Lt. co. M., N. Y. Lincoln Cavalry

NORTON, JOHN R. (Veteran). Enlisted in co. K, N. Y. Lincoln cav. as corporal, Aug. 12, 1861, at Grand Rapids, for 3 yrs.

Age 23.

Mustered, Aug. 12, 1861.

Re-enlisted, Jan. 1, 1864, at Charleston, Va. Mustered, Jan. 1, 1864.

Commissioned 2nd lt., Dec. 7, 1864, to rank from Sept. 30, 1864.

Mustered out at Alexandria, Va., June 27, 1865.

Medal of Honor award:—Lieut. John R. Norton, co. M, 1st N. Y. (Lincoln) cav., was awarded a Congressional Medal of Honor, May 3, 1865, for the capture of a flag, April 6, 1865, at Sailors Creek, Va.

HENRY C. PETERS, M. H.
Co. B, 47th Ohio Infantry

PETERS, HENRY C. (Veteran). Enlisted in co. B, 47th Ohio, June 15, 1861, for 3 yrs.

Age 21.

Re-enlisted, Feb. 20, 1864, at Cleveland, Tenn. Mustered, Mar. 6, 1864.

Promoted cor., Nov. 1, 1864.

Sergeant, Jan. 1, 1865.

Missing, July 13, 1865.

Medal of Honor award:—Henry C. Peters, pvt. co. B, 47th Ohio inf. vols., was awarded a Congressional Medal of Honor, April 17, 1917, for gallantry in action at Vicksburg, Miss., May 3, 1863.

HENRY E. PLANT, M. H.
Corp. co. F., 14th Mich Infantry.

PLANT, HENRY E. (Veteran), Crockery. Enlisted in
co. F, 14th Mich. inf., Dec. 5, 1861, at Crockery for
3 years.
Age 21.
Mustered, Feb. 13, 1862.
Re-enlisted, Jan. 4, 1864, at Franklin, Tenn.
Mustered, Feb. 5, 1864.
Sergeant.
Mustered out at Louisville, Ky., July 18, 1865.
Later residence, Nunica, Mich.
Medal of Honor award:—Conferred by War dept.,
April 27, 1896. At Bentonville, N. C., on the 19th
of Mar., 1865, Corp. Henry E. Plant, co. F, 14th
Mich. "rushed into the midst of the enemy and
rescued the colors, the bearer having fallen mortally
wounded."

GEORGE E. RANNEY, M. H.
Asst. Surgeon, 2nd Mich. Cavalry

RANNEY, GEORGE E., Charlotte.   Entered service as
private, Sept. 9, 1861, in 2nd cav., at Grand Rapids,
for 3 yrs.
Age 23.
Mustered as Hospital Steward, Oct. 2, 1861.
Honorably discharged for disability at Cincinnati, Ohio,
July 16, 1862.
Re-entered service in 2nd cav. as assistant surgeon.
Commissioned, June 6, 1863.   Mustered, June 6, 1863.
Commissioned surgeon, Nov. 15, 1864.   Mustered,
Nov. 25, 1864.

Appointed surgeon 136th U. S. colored troops. Dis-
charged at Augusta, Ga., Jan. 1, 1866.
Served as active assistant surgeon while at Hospital
Steward.
May 9, 1864, was made brigade surgeon by special
order of medical director for bravery and efficiency
in action on battle field.
Served in the dual role of brigade surgeon and surgeon
of his regiment in Sherman campaign, 1864.
Promoted surgeon 2nd cav., Nov. 15, 1864.
Surgeon of first division cav. corps, military division
of the Mississippi, Feb. 27, 1865.
May 1, 1865, placed in charge of the consolidated di-
vision hospital corps.
Awarded Medal of Honor by Congress for most dis-
tinguished gallantry at Resaca, Ga., May 14, 1864.
Taken prisoner at Chickamauga, Sept. 20, 1863.
Sent to Libby prison. Released, Nov. 24, 1863.
Dec., 1863 was assigned duty at Nashville, Tenn., where
he organized and managed "Convalescent Camp
Smith."
Took part in campaigns and engagements to the end
of the Civil War.
Later residence, Lansing, Mich.
Medal of Honor award:—May 14, 1864. "At great
personal danger went to the aid of a wounded soldier
lying under heavy fire between lines and with the
aid of an orderly carried him to a place of safety."
Awarded, Apr. 24, 1901.

JAMES H. ROBINSON, M. H.
3rd Mich. Cavalry

ROBINSON, JAMES H. Victor. Enlisted in co. B, 3rd
cav., Feb. 22, 1864, at Corunna, for 3 yrs.

Age 18.

Mustered, Feb. 22, 1864.

Died at Memphis, Tenn., grave 4131.

Medal of Honor award:—James H. Robinson, pvt. co.
B, 3rd Mich. cav., was awarded Congressional Medal
of Honor. "Successfully defended himself single-
handed against seven guerillas, killing the leader and
driving off the remainder of the party." Awarded
Apr. 4, 1865.

HENRY TECUMSEH ROMEYN, M. H.
Lt. 5th U. S. Infantry

ROMEYN, HENRY TECUMSEH.

Private, 1862.

Corporal co. 105th Ill. vol., Aug. 15, 1862.

Sergt., Mar., 1, 1862.

Capt. 14th U. S. colored troops, Nov. 15, 1863.

Brevet maj. vol., Mar. 13, 1865, for gallant and meritorious conduct in the battle of Nashville, Tenn.

Mustered out, Mar. 26, 1866.

1st lt. 37th U. S. army, Jan. 22, 1867.

Brevet capt. U. S. army, Mar. 2, 1867, for gallant
and meritorious conduct in the battle of Nashville,
Tenn.

Unassigned, May 19, 1869.

Assigned to 5th inf., Aug. 14, 1869.

Capt., July 10, 1865.

Awarded Medal of Honor, Nov. 27, 1894.

Retired, June 1, 1897.

Medal of Honor award:—Henry Romeyn, 1st lt. 5th
U. S. inf., was awarded the Congressional Medal of
Honor for most distinguished gallantry in action
against hostile Nez Perce Indians, at Bear Paw Mt.,

Mont., Sept. 30, 1877, in leading his command into close range of the enemy there maintaining his position and vigorously prosecuting the fight until he was severely wounded.

CHARLES F. SANSCRAINTE, M. H.
15th Mich. Infantry

SANSCRAINTE. CHARLES F., Monroe County. Enlisted in co. B, 15th inf., Dec. 24, 1861, at Monroe for 3 yrs.
Age 20.
Mustered, Jan. 29, 1863.
Discharged at expiration of service at Ft. McAllister, Ga., Dec. 24, 1864.
A resolution presented to Mich. Legislature, 1865, recommending Medal of Honor "for distinguished gallantry and personal bravery at Atlanta, where he mounted the breastworks of the enemy and gave signal to Col. LaPoint to charge. In this charge Sanscrainte in a hand to hand fight captured the colors of the 5th Texas but received two gun wounds and a bayonet wound in the contest for the colors. He was in every battle with his regiment from Pittsburg Landing, Tenn., in Apr. 1862, until the capture of Ft. McAllister, Ga., Dec., 1864, and was in the advance guard at Ft. McAllister when that stronghold was stormed and captured."
Later residence, Trenton, N. J.
Medal of Honor award:—July 25, 1892. Charles F. Sanscrainte, July 22, 1864, at Atlanta "Voluntarily scaled the enemy's works and signaled to his commanding officer to charge; also, in single combat captured colors of 5th Texas reg."

EDWIN F. SAVACOOL, M. H.
Capt. co. K, Lincoln Cavalry

SAVACOOL, EDWIN F. Enlisted in co. K, N. Y. Lincoln
cavalry, organized at Grand Rapids, Mich., and
mustered into U. S. service, Aug. 12, 1861. Enlisted
at Grand Rapids for 3 yrs.
Age 21.
Mustered, Aug. 29, 1861.
Commissioned 2nd lt., July 27, 1864.
Commissioned capt., Jan. 27, 1865 to rank from Dec.
1, 1864.
Died at Washington, D. C., June 3, 1865, from wounds
received in action at Sailors Creek, Va., Apr. 6,
1865.
Medal of Honor award:—Edwin F. Savacool, capt. co.
K, 1st N. Y. Lincoln cav., was awarded Congressional Medal of Honor, Apr. 24, 1865, for capture of
flag, Apr. 6, 1865, at Sailors Creek, Va.

WILLIAM R. SHAFTER, M. H.
Lieut. co. I, 7th Mich. Infantry.

SHAFTER, WILLIAM RUFUS. Born Galesburg, Mich.,
Oct. 16, 1835.
Son of Hugh M. and Eliza (Sumner) Shafter.
Educated in common schools.
Married Sept. 11, 1862, Harriet Grimes, of Athens,
Mich., who died Jan. 14, 1898.
Entered service in co. I, 7th inf., at organization, as
1st lieut., June 28, 1861, at Ft. Wayne, for three
years.
Age 26.
Commissioned, June 28, 1861. Mustered, Aug. 22,
1861.

Major 19th Mich. inf., Sept. 5, 1862.

Lt. col. June 5, 1863.

Col. 17th U. S. colored inf., April 19, 1864.

Brevet brig. gen., Mar. 13, 1865, for gallant and meritorious services during war.

Mustered out of service, Nov. 2, 1865.

Entered regular army as lieut. col., Jan. 26, 1867.

Brevet col. U. S. army, Mar. 2, 1867 and given Congressional Medal of Honor for gallant and meritorious service at battle of Fair Oaks, Va.

Transferred to 24th inf., April 14, 1869.

Col., Mar. 4, 1879.

Transferred to 1st inf., brig. gen., May 3, 1897, in charge of dep't of Calif.

Maj. gen. volunteers, May, 1898.

Transferred to Tampa, Fla.

Transferred to Cuba where he commanded the military operations ending in capitulation of Gen. Lenares' army and the surrender of Santiago de Cuba, July, 1898.

Commanded dep't of Calif., and Columbia, 1899–1901.

Retired, June 30, 1901, as major general.

Later residence, Bakersfield, Calif.

Died, 1906.

Medal of Honor award:—June 12, 1895, for most distinguished gallantry in battle of Fair Oaks, Va., May 31, 1862. While serving as first lieut. co. L, 7th inf., in command of pioneers, voluntarily taking an active part in the battle and remaining on the field, although wounded, until the close of the engagement.

IRWIN P. SHEPHARD, M. H.
Corp. co. E, 17th Mich. Infantry

SHEPHARD, IRWIN P., Chelsea. Enlisted in co. E, 17th inf., Aug. 7, 1862, at Ypsilanti for 3 yrs.
Age 19.
Mustered, Aug. 19, 1862. Corporal. Wounded in action at Wilderness, Va., May 22, 1864.
1st sergt. Apr. 13, 1865. Discharged at Detroit, May 22, 1865.
Granted Medal of Honor for gallantry at Knoxville, Tenn.
Later residence, Winona, Wis.
Medal of Honor award:—Irwin Shephard, corp. co. E, 17th Mich. inf., was awarded Medal of Honor by War department for gallantry in action at Knoxville, Tenn., Nov. 20, 1863. "Having voluntarily accompanied a small party to destroy buildings within the enemy's lines, when sharpshooters had been firing—disregarded an order to retire, remained and completed the firing of the buildings thus insuring their total destruction this at the imminent risk of his life from the fire of the advancing enemy."

GEORGE D. SIDMAN, M. H.
Drummer 16th Mich. Infantry

SIDMAN, GEORGE D., Wayne Co. Enlisted in co. C, 16th inf., as drummer, Aug. 1, 1861, at Flint for 3 yrs.
Age 18.
Mustered, Sept. 7, 1861.
Wounded and taken prisoner at Gaines Mills, Va., June 27, 1862.

Corporal.

Wounded in action, June 27, 1862.

Transferred to invalid corps, Dec. 9, 1863.

Discharged, Nov. 14, 1865, from co. D, 12th regiment veteran reserve corps.

Medal of Honor award:—Geo. D. Sidman, pvt., co. C, 16th Mich. inf., was awarded Congressional Medal of Honor for distinguished bravery in battle at Gaines Mills, Va., June 27, 1862. Medal of Honor awarded, Apr. 6, 1892.

ALONZO SMITH, M. H.
Sergt. co. C, 7th Mich. Infantry

SMITH, ALONZO, Veteran. Jonesville. Enlisted in co. C, 7th inf., Aug. 9, 1861, at Jonesville, for 3 yrs.

Age 19.

Mustered, Aug. 22, 1861.

Wounded in action at Antietam, Md., Sept. 17, 1862.

Corp., Jan., 1863.

Wounded in action at Gettysburg, Pa., July 2, 1863.

Re-enlisted, Dec. 16, 1863, at Stevensburg, Va. Mustered, Dec. 19, 1863.

1st lt. June 12, 1864. Mustered, Jan. 7, 1865.

Mustered out at Jeffersonville, Ind., July 5, 1865.

Medal of Honor award:—Alonzo Smith, serg. co. C, 7th Mich. inf.

Date of issue:—Dec. 1, 1864.

Place of action:—Hatchers Run, Va.

Time of action:—Oct. 27, 1864.

Ground of award:—Capture of flag of 26th N. C. inf., C. S. A.

Report by Lieut. Col. Horace P. Rugg of the 59th N. Y. volunteers, commanding brigade to Lieut. Wm. H. Gilder, acting asst. adj. gen. "I beg leave to

mention for especial gallantry Geo. W. LaPoint, 7th
Mich. vol., for fighting way through enemy's cavalry,
on the morning of the 28th and Sergt. Alonzo Smith, co.
C, 7th Mich. vol., for capturing the colors of the 26th
N. C. (rebel) regiment." *War of the Rebellion*, Vol.
42, p. 304.

The companies of the 7th were recruited in different
parts of the state and the regiment was mustered into
service Aug. 22, 1861, at Monroe.   It was composed of
the Union Guard of Port Huron; Cirtenius Guard of
Mason; Jonesville Light Guard of Jonesville; Monroe
Light Guards of Monroe; Tuscola vol. of Tuscola;
Blair Guards of Farmington; Lapeer Guards of Lapeer;
one company from Pontiac; Prairieville Rangers of
Prairieville; and Burr Oak Rangers of Burr Oak.   The
7th left Monroe, Sept. 5, 1861, under the command of
Col. Ira R. Grosvenor and joined the Army of the
Potomac.   Officers were: Col. Ira E. Grosvenor, Mon-
roe; Lt. Col. Frazy N. Winas; Maj. Nath. R. Eldridge,
Lapeer; Surgeon Bolivar Barnum, Schoolcraft; Adj.
Harry B. Landon, Monroe; Qm. Charles M. Walker,
Lapeer.   Company C, Capt. Harry Baxter, Jonesville;
1st Lt. Sidney B. Voorman, Jonesville; 2nd Lt.
Harry B. Landon, Monroe.

In the spring of 1862 the regiment was assigned to the
3rd brigade, 2nd division, 2nd corps.

"The regiment was noted for its steadiness under
fire, for its gallantry in action and its stubborn resistance
confronting the enemy."

FREDERICK W. SWIFT, M. H.
Lt. Col. 17th Mich. Infantry

SWIFT, FREDERICK W., Detroit.   Entered service in co.
F, 17th inf., at organization, as captain, July 29,
1862 at Detroit, for 3 yrs.

Age 31.

Commissioned to date, June 17, 1862. Mustered, Aug. 26, 1862.

Commissioned lieut. col., Nov. 26, 1863. Mustered, Jan. 13, 1864.

Commanding regiment, Nov. 25, 1863.

Taken prisoner at Spottsylvania, Va., May 12, 1864.

Returned to regiment, Aug. 3, 1864.

On staff of Gen. Wilcox, Oct., 1864.

Commissioned colonel, Dec. 4, 1864.

Mustered out and honorably discharged at DeLaney House, D. C., June 3, 1865.

Brevet brigade gen. U. S. volunteers, Mar. 13, 1865, for gallant and meritorious conduct during the war.

Medal of Honor awarded by War dep't, Feb. 15, 1897.

Later residence, Detroit.

Medal of Honor award:—Nov. 16, 1863, at Lenoir Station, Tenn., Lieut. Col. Frederick W. Swift, 17th Mich. inf., "gallantly seized the colors and rallied the regiment after three color bearers had been shot, and the regiment having become demoralized was in imminent danger of capture.

"I cannot speak in too high terms of all the officers and men of my regiment but will mention some who are especially deserving of notice. I am greatly indebted to Capt. F. W. Swift (acting major), Capt. John Tyler, and Adj. R. A. Watts for their brave, gallant and efficient conduct during the entire day." Lieut. Col. Comstock to Lieut. B. H. Berry, acting adj. gen., report Nov. 21, 1863. See also, Joseph E. Brandle.

PETER SYPE, M. H.
Co. B, 47th Ohio Infantry

SYPE, PETER, pvt. in co. B, 47th Ohio inf. (A Mich. company organized by W. H. Ward of Adrian). Enlisted in co. B, 47th Ohio inf., June 15, 1861, for 3 yrs.

Age 20.

Discharged at end of term of service at Atlanta, Ga., Sept. 10, 1864.

Medal of Honor award:—For gallantry of action at Vicksburg, Miss., May, 1863. "Was one of a party that volunteered and attempted to run the enemy's batteries with a steam tug and two barges loaded with subsistence stores."

CHAS. M. THATCHER, M. H.
1st Mich. Sharpshooters

THATCHER, CHAS. M., Eastmanville. Enlisted in co. B, 1st S. S., Dec. 5, 1862, at Grand Haven for 3 yrs.

Age 18.

Taken prisoner at Petersburg, Va., July 30, 1864.

Returned to regiment, Apr. 1, 1865.

Discharged at Washington, D. C., July 1, 1865.

Died, Dec. 13, 1900.

Buried at Kalkaska, Mich.

Medal of Honor award:—July 30, 1864 at Petersburg, Va., Chas. M. Thatcher, pvt. co. B, 1st Mich. S. S., "Instead of retreating or surrendering when the works were captured, regardless of personal safety, continued to return the enemy fire until captured." Awarded, July 31, 1896.

CHAS. A. THOMPSON, M. H.
Sergt. co. D, 17th Mich. Infantry

THOMPSON, CHAS. A. Enlisted in co. D, 17th inf., as corp., June 9, 1862, at Kalamazoo for 3 yrs.
Age 19.
Mustered, June 30, 1862.
Sergt., Feb. 3, 1865. Discharged to accept promotion, May 1, 1865.
Commissioned 2nd lieut., co. H, April 25, 1865.
Mustered, May 2, 1865.
Mustered out at DeLaney House, D. C., June 3, 1865.
July 27, 1896, was granted Medal of Honor for gallantry at Spottsylvania, Va. Died at Rutland, Vt., Aug. 24, 1900.
Medal of Honor award:—Chas. A. Thompson, Sergt. co. D, 17th Mich. inf., was awarded the Medal of Honor by the War dep't July 27, 1896. May 12, 1864, at Spottsylvania, Va., after the regiment was surrounded and all resistance seemed useless, fought singlehanded for colors and refused to give them up until he had appealed to his superior officers.
See report by Lieut. Col. L. L. Comstock (commanding regiment) *War of Rebellion*, Series 1, XXXIII, 367. "Chas. Thompson carrier of the State colors was equally gallant and called upon the men to stand firmly by the standard he bore."

JAMES W. TOBAN, M. H.
Sergt. co. C, 9th Mich. Cavalry

TOBAN, JAMES W., Northfield. Enlisted in co. C, 9th cavalry, Nov. 10, 1862, at Northfield, for 3 yrs.
Age 18.
Mustered, Jan. 22, 1863.

Sergt., Nov. 1, 1864.

Commissioned 2nd lieut., June 27, 1865.

Mustered out at Lexington, N. C., July 21, 1865.

Received Medal of Honor from the govt. for conspicuous bravery at Aiken, S. C.

Died at Lansing, Mich., Nov. 1, 1903.

Buried at Northfield, Mich.

Medal of Honor award:—The War dep't awarded the
Medal of Honor to James W. Toban, sergt. co. C, 9th
Mich. cav., July 9, 1896.

Ground of award:—"Feb. 11, 1865, James W. Toban
voluntarily, and at great personal risk, returned in
the face of the enemy and rescued from impending
death or capture Major C. Stevens, 9th Mich. cav.,
who had been thrown from his horse."

ANDREW TRAYNOR, M. H.
Corp. co. D, 1st Mich. Cavalry

TRAYNOR, ANDREW, Sciota.   Enlisted in co. D, 1st
cav., Aug. 12, 1861, at Ovid, for 3 yrs.

Age 19.

Mustered, Sept. 6, 1861.

Discharged at expiration of term of service at Washington, D. C., Aug. 24, 1864.

Later residence, Council Bluffs, Iowa.

"Corp. Traynor, co. D, 1st Mich. cavalry.

"Corporal: The Maj. Gen. commanding the Dept.
desires me to thank you for the gallant and soldierly
conduct by which you liberated yourself and comrades
while disarmed and in the hands of armed guerillas.
The same manly spirit and action shown by you if
manifested by your comrades would rid the Dept. of

the predatory bands calling themselves Confederate
soldiers.

"Very respectfully,
J. H. Taylor,
Chief of staff, A. A. G."

Medal of Honor award:—At Masons Hill, Va., Mar.
16, 1864, Andrew Traynor, Corp. co. D, 1st cav.,
"Having been surprised and captured by a detachment of guerillas, this soldier with other prisoners,
seized the arms of the guard over them killed two of
the guerillas and enabled all the prisoners to escape."
Award made by Congress, Sept. 28, 1897.

WILLIAM H. WARD, M. H.
Co. B, 47th Ohio Infantry

WARD, WILLIAM H., Capt. co. B, 47th Ohio inf.   En-
tered service in co. B, 47th Ohio, at organization, as
Capt., June 15, 1861, at Adrian for 3 yrs.
Age 27.
Commissioned, Aug. 28, 1861.   Mustered, July 29,
1861.
Discharged at expiration of term of service, Aug. 9,
1864.
Medal of Honor award:—William H. Ward, pvt. co.
B, 47th Ohio inf., Jan. 2, 1893, was awarded Medal
of Honor, at Vicksburg, Miss., for action May 3, 1863.
Ground of award:—"Voluntarily commanded the ex-
pedition which, under cover of darkness, attempted
to run the enemy's batteries."
Co. B, 47th Ohio inf. (A company organized at
Adrian by Wm. H. Ward and accepted for service by
Gov. of Ohio.)

LOYD WHEATON, M. H.

Lieut. Colonel 8th Illinois Infantry

WHEATON, LOYD, major general U. S. A.

Born at Pennfield, Mich., July 15, 1838.

Son of William G. and Amanda M. (Parker) Wheaton.

Married Mrs. Charlotte Flower Derby of N. Y., Dec. 17, 1867, who died Oct. 20, 1905. She was a descendant of Gov. Wm. Bradford, Plymouth, Mass.

Enlisted as 1st sergt. co. E, 8th Illinois inf., April 20, 1861.

Discharged July 24, 1861.

Commissioned 1st lieut., 8th Illinois inf., July 25, 1861.

Captain, Mar. 25, 1862.

Major, Aug. 28, 1863.

Wounded at Shiloh.

Lieut. col., Nov. 25, 1864.

Honorably mustered out, May 4, 1866.

Appointed from Illinois, capt. 34th U. S. inf., July 28, 1866.

Assigned to 20th inf., Sept. 1, 1869.

Major, Oct. 14, 1891.

Lieut. col., May 31, 1895.

Transferred to 20th inf., Sept. 11, 1895.

Brig. gen. volunteers, May 27, 1898.

Transferred to 2nd U. S. inf., Dec. 30, 1898.

Col. 20th inf., Feb. 6, 1899.

Honorably discharged from volunteer service, Apr. 15, 1899, with rank of brigadier-general.

Transferred to 7th U. S. inf., Feb. 3, 1900.

Major gen. volunteers, June 18, 1900.

Brig. gen. U. S. A., Feb. 2, 1901.

Honorably discharged from volunteer service, Feb. 28, 1901.

Maj. general U. S. A., Mar. 30, 1901.

Retired by operation of law, July 15, 1902.

Breveted major, Mar. 2, 1867, "for gallant and meritorious services in siege of Vicksburg, Miss."

Lieut. col Mar. 2, 1867, for the same, in assault on Ft. Blakely, Ala.

Col. volunteers, Mar. 26, 1865, for same during campaign against Mobile.

Maj. gen. volunteers, June 19, 1899, for gallantry in action against insurgents near Inius, P. I.

In service at western and other posts to 1898.

Commanded division of 7th army corps, Spanish-Amer. war.

Participated in all principal battles and combats in P. I., 1899–1902.

Commanded departments northern Luzon and North Philippines, 1900–2.

Later residence:—2738 Pine Grove ave., Chicago, Ill.

Medal of Honor award:—Jan. 16, 1894, awarded Medal of Honor by Congress "for distinguished gallantry in assault on Ft. Blakely, Ala., April 9, 1865, leading right wing of his regiment, springing through an embrasure against a strong fire of artillery and musketry and first to enter enemy's works."

WILLIAM G. WHITNEY, M. H.
Lieut. co. B, 11th Mich. Infantry

WHITNEY, WILLIAM G., Allen. Enlisted in co. B, 11th inf., as sergt., Aug. 24, 1861, at Allen, for 3 yrs. Age 21.

Mustered, Aug. 24, 1861.

Commissioned 2nd lieut., Jan. 7, 1863.

Commissioned 1st lieut., June 17, 1864.

Mustered, July 17, 1864.

Transferred to reorganized co. B, 11th inf., Feb. 15, 1865.

Commissioned capt., Mar. 1, 1865.

Mustered, Apr. 11, 1865.

Mustered out at Nashville, Tenn., Sept. 16, 1865.

Later residence, Allen, Mich.

Wounded in action; received Medal of Honor for gallantry of action at Chickamauga, Ga.

Medal of Honor award:—Sept. 20, 1863, "As the enemy was about to charge this officer went outside the temporary Union works among the dead and wounded enemy and at great exposure to himself cut off and removed their cartridge boxes bringing the same within the Union lines; the ammunition being used with good effect in repulsing the attack." Awarded, Oct. 21, 1895.

ORLANDO B. WILLCOX, M. H.
Colonel 1st Michigan Infantry

Willcox, Orlando Bolivar.   Born in Detroit, April 16, 1823.   Son of Charles and Almira Willcox.

Graduated West Point, 1847.

Fought in Mexican, Seminole, and the other Indian campaigns and in the Civil War.   Service with the 4th U.S. artillery, 1st Mich. volunteers, 12th and 29th regulars; commanded several military depots and the Soldiers' Home.

Author of "Shorpac Recollections" by Walter March, 1854.

Later residence, Washington.

Military service:—Military Academy, West Point, 1843.

WILLIAM H. WITHINGTON,
Brevet Brigadier General, U. S. Volunteers.

2nd lieut. 4th U. S. artillery, July 1, 1847. Resigned Sept. 30, 1850.

1st lieut., April 30, 1850.

Entered volunteer service in 1st inf. as a colonel, Apr. 24, 1861, for three months.

Age 38.

Commissioned and mustered, May 1, 1861.

Prisoner at Bull Run, July 21, 1861.

Exchanged, Aug. 17, 1862.

Appointed brig. gen., July 21, 1861.

Mustered out and honorably discharged, Aug. 16, 1862.

Breveted maj. gen. U. S. volunteers, Aug. 1, 1864, "for distinguished and gallant service in the several actions since crossing the Rapidan."

Mustered out and honorably discharged, Jan. 15, 1866.

Commissioned colonel 29th U. S. inf., July 28, 1866.

Breveted brig. gen. U. S. A., Mar. 2, 1867.

Retired, April 16, 1877.

Medal of Honor award:—Orlando Bolivar Willcox, col. 1st Mich. inf., was awarded Congressional Medal of Honor, Mar. 2, 1895. "At Bull Run, Va., July 21, 1861, led repeated charges until wounded and taken prisoner."

WILLIAM H. WITHINGTON, M. H.
Capt. co. B., 1st Michigan Infantry

Withington, William Herbert. Born at Dorchester, Mass., Feb., 1835.

Son of William and Elizabeth W. (Ford) Withington. Descended from Henry Withington, who came from England in 1735, with the Reverend Richard Mather.

Education:—Educated in the public schools of Boston and at Andover Academy.

Captain of the Jackson Grays which he helped to organize. The Grays answered Lincoln's first call for troops and became co. B, 1st Michigan volunteer infantry.

Civil War service:—Entered service in co. B, 1st Mich. inf., as captain, April 29, 1861, at Jackson, for three years.

Age 26.

Commissioned May 1, 1861. Mustered, May 1, 1861.

Wounded and taken prisoner at Bull Run, Va., July 21, 1861.

Exchanged, Jan. 30, 1862.

Commissioned col. 17th inf. at organization, Aug. 11, 1862.

Mustered, Aug. 21, 1862.

Commanded 1st brigade, Oct. 16-28, 1862.

Commanded 2nd brigade, 1st division, 9th army corps, Nov., 1862.

Returned to regiment, Dec. 21, 1862.

Resigned and honorably discharged, Mar. 21, 1863.

Brevet brig. gen. U. S. volunteers, Mar. 13, 1865, for conspicuous gallantry at the battle of South Mountain, Md., Sept. 14, 1862.

Married Julia C., dau. of Joseph E. Beebe, June 6, 1859.

Children:—Philip H.; Winthrop Jackson; and Kate Winifred, wife of Dr. Flemming Carrow, Traverse City, Mich.

Elected to legislature, 1873. Was the originator of a bill providing for the creation of an effective State militia; became colonel 1879; was appointed brigadier general. Resigned, 1883.

Elected State senator, 1891-2.

Member of State Central Committee (Republican).

Died at Jackson, Mich., June 27, 1903.
Medal of Honor award:—

"Record and Pension Office
War Department Office.

"Washington, D. C.,
Jan. 7, 1895.

"General Wm. H. Withington,
Jackson, Michigan.
"Sir:—

"I have the honor to inform you that by direction of
the President and in accordance with the Act of Congress, approved March 3, 1863, providing for the pre-
sentation of Medals of Honor to such officers, non-
commissioned officers and privates as have most distinguished themselves in action, the Assistant Secretary of War has awarded you a Medal of Honor, for
most distinguished gallantry, in voluntarily remaining
on the field under heavy fire, to aid and succor
your superior officer in the Battle of Bull Run, Va.,
July 21, 1861.

"Very respectfully,
Colonel ————
U. S. Army.

"Chief Record and Pension Office."

BENJAMIN F. YOUNGS, M. H.
Corp. co. I, 1st Mich. S. S.

YOUNGS, BENJAMIN F. Enlisted in co. I, 1st S. S., Sept.,
1863, at Detroit, for 3 yrs.
Age 19.
Mustered, Sept. 4, 1863.
Promoted corp., June 20, 1864.

Promoted to sergt. for distinguished gallantry before
Petersburg on the 17th of June, 1864, capturing the
colors of the 35th N. C. regiment, by S. O. No. 20
of the 9th army corps dated June 20, 1864.

Missing in action, Sept. 30, 1864.

Medal of Honor award:—Dec. 1, 1864, Benjamin F.
Youngs, was awarded Congressional Medal of Honor
for gallantry of action June 17, 1864 at Petersburg,
Va.

Ground of award:—Capture of flag of 35th N. C. inf.
(C. S. A.).

MICHIGAN MEN IN THE GREAT WAR

General John Pershing's Tribute to the American Army in France, Among Whom Were the 32nd and Many Other Michigan Troops.

WITH the American Army in France, Aug. 27, 1918.

Gen. John J. Pershing, commander-in-chief of the American army in France, issued the following order:

"It fills me with pride to record in general orders a tribute to the service achievements of First and Third Corps, comprising the First, Second, Third, Fourth, Twenty-sixth, Twenty-eignth, Thirty-second and Forty-second divisions of American Expeditionary Forces.

"You came to the battle-field at a crucial hour for the Allied cause. For almost four years, the most formidable army the world has yet seen had pressed its invasion of France and stood threatening its capitol.

"At no time has that army been more powerful and menacing than when, on July 15, 1918, it struck again to destroy in one great battle, the brave men opposed to it and to enforce its brutal will upon the world and civilization.

"Three days later in conjunction with our Allies you counter-attacked. The Allied armies began a brilliant victory that marks the turning point of the war. You did more than give the Allies the support to which, as a nation our faith was pledged. You proved that our altruism, our pacific spirit and our sense of justice have not blunted our virility or our courage.

"You have shown that American initiative and energy are as fit for the tasks of war as for the pursuits of peace. You have justly won unstinted praise from our Allies and the eternal gratitude of our countrymen.

"We have paid for our success with the lives of many of our brave comrades. We shall cherish their memory always and claim for our history and literature their bravery, achievement and sacrifice.

"This order will be read to all organizations at the first assembly formations following its receipt."

GENERAL INDEX

www.ingramcontent.com/pod-product-compliance
Lightning Source LLC
Chambersburg PA
CBHW061006280326
41935CB00009B/859